CW01021129

BLAKWIDOW

BLAKWIDOW

MY FIRST YEAR
AS A PROFESSIONAL
WRESTLER

AMANDA STORM

ECW PRESS

I would like to dedicate this effort to my loving husband, Donald,
who has given up so much for what has seemed at times like
a cruel pipedream. But we have stayed the course,
weathered some rough seas and some very good
things are starting to finally happen.
I love you flippors!

Copyright © ECW PRESS, 2000

All rights reserved. No part of this publication may be reproduced, stored in a retrieval
system, or transmitted in any form by any process — electronic, mechanical, photocopying,
recording, or otherwise — without the prior written permission of ECW PRESS.

CANADIAN CATALOGUING IN PUBLICATION DATA

Storm, Amanda
Blakwidow : my first year as a professional wrestler

ISBN 1-55022-431-X

1. Storm, Amanda.   2. Women wrestlers — United States — Biography.   I. Title.

GV1196.S76A3 2000   796.812'092   C00-931717-1

Edited by Jennifer Hale
Cover and text design by Tania Craan
Layout by Mary Bowness
Front cover photo: Photography by Brown
Back cover photos: D.J. vonWyc
Printed by AGMV

Distributed in Canada by General Distribution Services, 325 Humber Blvd., Toronto,
Ontario M9W 7C3. Distributed in the United States by LPC GROUP, 1436 West Randolph
Street, Chicago, Illinois, U.S.A. 60607. Distributed in Europe by Turnaround Publisher
Services, Unit 3, Olympia Trading Estate,Coburg Road, Wood Green, London N2Z 6TZ.
Distributed in Australia by Wakefield Press, 17 Rundle St., Kent Town, South Australia 5071.

Published by ECW PRESS
2120 Queen Street East, Suite 200,
Toronto, Ontario, M4E 1E2
ecwpress.com

The publication of *Blakwidow* has been generously supported by the Government of
Canada through the Book Publishing Industry Development Program.

Canadä

PRINTED IN CANADA

TABLE OF CONTENTS

FOREWORD

The first time I met Amanda Storm, I just saw her as just another girl. And then I put her in the ring with a bunch of other guys. At first we make them walk around the ring and say the names of the other wrestlers and look menacing, but she just jumped in and started screaming! Cussing this guy, swearing at that guy and we all looked at her and thought, Holy mackerel. She just surprised us all, she really did. She picks up things very quickly. I'll show her a move, and she'll pick it up right away. Every time she comes back to the school I'll show her something else and she'll say, "Oh, I like that one," and she uses it in her act right away. She really surprised me.

In the ring she tends to be the villain and she plays the part very well. She goes to that ring, looks at the opponent and just shouts, "I'll smash you!" and then she goes ahead and has a great match. She lets the people know who she is and lets them know she's the BEST (whether they agree with her or not). She'll just yell at her opponent and the audience things like, "You come near me and I'll break your neck!" Everyone knows who Amanda Storm is when she's wrestling. She's a great actress, though, because in person she's very nice (which is why she surprised me so much the first time she stepped into the ring).

I see her going a long way in the future. At this time, she's doing very very well, and she's a very good performer in the ring. I think she'll go far, depending on herself. I've been showing her new moves that she's been using in different cities, and she catches on quickly every time. If she keeps progressing the way she has so far, she'll go as far as she wants to go.

Walter "Killer" Kowalski
September 2000

GLOSSARY

BABYFACE: By definition the exact opposite of Amanda Storm. Seriously, a babyface wrestler is a "fan favorite." She slaps hands with the people, tries to play by the rules, and all in all is a good girl. Enough to make you want to run out and vomit.

BACKDROP: The heel bends over as Amanda is running at him, and she flips way up in the air and lands on her back. That is the theory in any case.

BASEBALL SLIDE: A motion where you run and then slide into your opponent much like a runner sliding into second base. This move is commonly done when the attacking wrestler is standing in the ring and her opponent is on the outside near the apron. In this situation the sliding wrestler catches the other wrestler right in the chest. I happened to have played a lot of softball so I'm particularly good at this move. I also do this move to guys when they are in the corner. I tell them to spread their legs when they are selling in the corner and of course I baseball slide into their crotch. Crowds love it.

BIRD: This is an honor you most definitely want to pass up. The bird in a battle royale is the person who everyone picks on, especially, it seems, with chops. The first and only time I was "the bird" I got chopped 57 times. Yes, I kept count.

BUM: A "bum" is a wrestler who the booker will use in the show if someone doesn't show up or gets hurt. Professional wrestling, like most things, requires equal amounts of preparation and being in the right place at the right time.

CHEAP HEAT: Eliciting a crowd response by using techniques such as sticking your middle finger up in the air and other vulgar gestures and expressions. The "Up Yours!" sign is my personal favorite, especially when I'm in foreign countries. I bet they'd just love Amanda Storm in Saudi Arabia.

FEUD: Amanda hates Violet and Violet hates Amanda. They pull each other's hair, they cost each other matches, they beat each other up, and take each other's lunch money. In other words you have two wrestlers who have a past history of bad blood which is a fertile ground to set up future matches. In professional wrestling this is a "feud." It is very much like when the announcers in football say, "These two teams don't like each other very much," to build excitement for the game by promising aggressive play and hard-hitting excitement because it isn't just a job, it's personal!

FIRING UP: A babyface will finally get tired of getting beaten up and will start screaming or waving her hands in some peculiar manner which translates to, "I'm sick of this crap and I'm not going to take it anymore!" She will then proceed to kick the snot out of the villain. This is the penultimate movement to the drama of most classic matches. From there comes victory or defeat.

GET OVER: Little Amanda is "getting over" when the fans love or hate her. If I am destroying some mindnumbingly sweet babyface and the fans fill the arena with boo's and catcalls when I stop to celebrate and flex a little, then I'm most definitely getting over. (See Heat.)

GIMMICK: Something that sets a wrestler apart, makes her (hopefully) unique, and helps make her more popular, either as a heel or face, with the fans. A gimmick can include a specific way of dressing, acting, or talking; a distinctive finishing move; and certain items one always carries to the ring. For example, I have an Evil American gimmick that I use up in Canada. I come to the ring waving a huge American flag and yell, "USA is number one!" and try to get them to cheer by clapping my hands in classic babyface style. The only problem is that I'm usually deep in the heart of Canada, and they hate me.

GIMMICKED: A prop that looks like the real deal but in fact is designed so it is safer, less dangerous, or at least not totally lethal. I have a number of "gimmicked" whips that look extremely mean and can be used to make a nice noise but in fact hardly hurt at all. Then again, I have some whips that look kind of bland and make very little noise but will literally tear holes in one's flesh. Naturally, I save the bland whips for people I don't like.

GO HOME: What the fans do when the show really sucks. Actually, "go home" means to wrap up a contest, go into the finish, and conclude the match. Often the referee relays this to the wrestlers, either by keeping track of the time that has been allotted or watching for a signal from a third party, such as the booker.

GLOSSARY

GOING OVER: Who gets to win in a contest where the victor is pre-determined. "Amanda is going over in her match with the Tuna Fish Assassin tonight on pay-per-view." In other words, Amanda has been pre-determined to win the match. (See Putting Over.)

GORILLA PRESS: This isn't an elegant move, but it's one where a wrestler showcases his strength by bodily hefting another wrestler over his head. Tony Atlas among others was famous for this move and used it on many people — including Hulk Hogan and yours truly — throughout his long and colorful career.

HAMMERLOCK: A hold where one wrestler grabs another wrestler by the wrist and forces her arm behind her back.

HEADLOCK: If you need me to tell you what this hold is, then you really should be thoroughly and truly ashamed. Bad toad!

HEAT: Heat equals excitement, pure and simple. You can have face heat and heel heat, which are appropriate crowd responses for what a wrestler is trying to portray in her performance. If I'm a heel then I want heel heat, which is the crowd booing and hating me. Face heat happens when the people respond with cheers and praise when I'm on top.

HEEL: The evil wrestler. She cheats, wins by shortcuts, and is usually an arrogant s.o.b. with no respect for the fans, other wrestlers, or herself. Naturally they are what truly makes rassling fun. After all, what would *Star Wars* be without Darth Vader?

HOPE SPOT: The heel is beating the crap out of the babyface, but the good girl comes back and gets a little offense before the heel stops her and goes back on the offense.

INDEPENDENT: This adjective refers to smaller wrestling promotions that aren't the "Big Three," i.e., the WWF, WCW, or ECW.

JOBBER: Professional loser. Some very good wrestlers, such as Iron Mike Sharpe and Barry Horowitz, have spent much of their careers as jobbers.

JOBBING: Being on the losing end in a match where the winner and loser is decided in the locker room before the show. "Amanda lost again tonight? She sure is jobbing a lot lately."

KAYFABE: Kayfabe is what this book isn't about — making believe that wrestling isn't a work. If kayfabe was still alive I would have never written this book. Why? Two reasons, the first is because I'd have too much respect for the corporate culture of professional wrestling to do such a thing and secondly out of fear. Wrestlers used to hurt other wrestlers who broke kayfabe. Now, in this era of Sports Entertainment, kayfabe is pretty much dead and people like me can call themselves performers and actually not get fitted for a neckbrace and concrete shoes.

LEG-DIVED: This is simply another way of saying that a wrestler shot in low and took another pugilist off her feet. Walter Kowalski has shown me several good ways to take much larger opponents off their feet, which has proven very useful to me because I have found that once I get even a very large man off his feet, his strength advantage (assuming he has one to begin with!) is often all but nullified.

LOCK UP: Two wrestlers come together and interlock their arms so they can test each other's strength as they move around the ring. This is the standard way to start a match, and is also called the "referee's position" or "tying up."

MARK: Technically a mark is a fan who thinks that wrestling is a "legitimate" sport, i.e., the outcomes are not predetermined and the apparent rules actually matter. More commonly this term is applied in a pejorative sense to people who are rabid fans, even if they understand something about how wrestling works. Personally I love marks — they are what makes wrestling fun.

MARK MAG: Magazines that present professional wrestling as a legitimate sport instead of legitimate sports entertainment. God bless them, each and every one, because they are great publicity for us independent workers.

MOONSAULT: A maneuver where a wrestler climbs to the top rope and jumps off with her back facing her opponent. But she does a backwards somersault in mid-air and lands on top of the other wrestler with a face-first splash. Very painful, of course. This move is problematic because the wrestlers often take so long to get into position that it looks overly contrived.

POP: A situation where the crowd responds with boo's or cheers to something they see during the show. I have "gotten a pop" in many ways — by insulting or complimenting the hometown, slinging around catch phrases with wild abandon, by pulling a can opener out of my bra during a match, or even by waving my arms around and acting silly before dropping a leg.

POTATO: A potato is a real shot that goes beyond merely being stiff. If someone punches me in the face and leaves a big bruise then I could say that he potatoed me.

PUTTING OVER: A verb meaning to lose on purpose. (See Going Over.)

REGISTER: This is selling, except not as long. Say I have someone hurt and they punch me in the stomach. I might react to it like it hurts, but only for a second and then I'm right back on the offense.

SELL: A wrestler "sells" a move when she reacts to a hold or move as if it were painful or difficult to escape from. This is otherwise known as "rolling around in your own vomit." (See Register.)

SIDE RUSSIAN LEG SWEEP: This is one of those moves in professional wrestling that I don't pretend to understand, even though I use it all the time, because you would think that it would do as much damage to the person using the move as it would to one's opponent. But, hey, this is pro wrestling, so such matters are really beside the point. I wrap my left arm around the other wrestler's shoulders, sort of like I'm giving him a friendly hug. At the same time I pull his left arm straight out across my chest, wrap my right leg around the front of his left leg and throw myself backwards so that both of us end up on our backs. Can you remember all of that? Don't feel bad; it took me a while to get it right, too!

SHOOT: Professional wrestling is a cooperative effort between two performers, like ballet. When one of the performers forgets this important fact and starts wrestling for real, he is said to be "shooting." There are many reasons why a wrestler might start shooting. The most common thing I have seen in the ring that have led to shoots are when one wrestler is overly stiff, which causes the other wrestler to lose his temper.

SIDEWALK SLAM: This is a good power move when someone is running full blast at poor little Amanda from behind. I catch him around the chest and left leg, using my opponent's momentum to lift him off his feet. From there I sit down, slamming him straight down into the mat. It is quite painful and very loud.

SPOT: A sequence of moves that the wrestlers arrange before or perhaps during a match. This is commonly done when they want to do something complicated or risky and it is essential they be on the same page at all times.

STIFF: The object of pro wrestling is to do things to your opponent that look painful. Some moves are going to hurt no matter what you do, but a skilled wrestler does her best to prevent unnecessary pain or injury to her opponent. Someone who works "stiff" is causing unnecessary pain. For example, instead of developing the skills necessary to throw a convincing-looking kick they simply kick their opponents. It looks painful because it is painful. (Also see Tight.)

SUNSET FLIP: Amanda's opponent shoots her off the ropes and bends over to give her a big backdrop. She leaps over his back while grabbing him around the waist. He ends up flat on his back for the pin.

TIGHT: A tight worker is one whose moves look convincing and might at times flirt with being stiff, but not usually in a bad or dangerous way. For example, you can feel a tight punch, but a stiff punch hurts.

WORKER: A "worker" is what we wrestlers call other wrestlers, especially ones who are at least reasonably skillful. It is often used as a term of respect or acceptance. Valets and managers are generally not granted this honorific.

WORKING: This term can have different shades of meaning, but in general it means to present something as if it were something else. Working can be like acting or lying, depending on the context. When I am kicking someone on the ground and those kicks look like they really hurt, then I'm working. If I tell another wrestler a fib she might say, "Stop working me, Amanda," which is to say that she thinks I'm not being totally honest with her.

INTRODUCTION

THE BLACK CURTAIN

STORMDATE: December, 1999.

I'm the chick waiting behind the black curtain. Perhaps you know me? That MTV honey with the red and black hair who said, "Character? What character? *Hijole madre*, I don't have no stinking character." The one with the blue swimsuit, an American flag in her hand, and the World Wrestling Federation heavyweight championship around her waist. (OK, so I made up that last part about the WWF, but I kind of like the sound of that somehow.)

"I'm Amanda Storm, I'm Amanda Storm in real life and what you see is what you get." Yup, that's what I told the folks at MTV and it's the stone cold truth. And there I was in Montreal on the snowy evening of December 27, 1999, for Jacques Rougeau's Lutte Internationale 2000 wrestling extravaganza. I often think about the sweat, the pain, and all the miles on the road that lead up to whatever black curtain I happen to be waiting behind on a given night. This night in Montreal was certainly no exception.

I had walked into Killer Kowalski's wrestling school exactly 372 days ago full of big hopes and even bigger fears. But in only 30 seconds I was going to walk into a ring surrounded by 2,700 screaming Canadian fans to defend my New England women's title. Well, one of my titles anyway. Was I nervous? Yes, but only a wee bit. This wasn't exactly my first time in front of a big crowd. But it was a long, strange, and sometimes painful 372 days leading up to this particular 15 minutes of fame . . .

I closed my eyes and took a deep breath as I ran over the opening of our match in my mind. Jacques had his hand clamped firmly around the nape of my neck. "Wait. Wait for it," he said, alternately loosening and tightening his grip on my neck.

The crowd was buzzing, and my latest theme music had a nice, heelish beat. What is more, I had dropped some weight, and for the first time in my life I was kind of pleased with how I looked in a bathing suit. No more baggy tank tops for "The Blakwidow" Amanda Storm!

"Now!" Rougeau yelled as he gave me a shove into that unforgiving limelight wrestlers crave. We small-time wrestlers get our fame in Warholian doses, one weekend at a time. We are stars of the moment, from the instant we step into that ring until we leave the building and drive off in our Yugos. In a way we are like shooting stars that burn brightly with the timekeeper's bell and wink out with the referee's 1-2-3. Then we go back to our lives as housewives, girlfriends, deli clerks, and software manual writers. Only to rise phoenix-like for another run the next Saturday night. Oh, and how we wrestlers crave that fiendish limelight. It is a drug, an intoxicant that we live for. More than money, sex, our personal lives, and even our health. Give it to me! Give it to me! Give it to me, baby!

I pranced down the runway waving my American flag, basking in the utter contempt and hatred of the fans. It was Quebec vs. America, so little Amanda Storm was the focus of everything that Canadians hate about the good old U S of A. I was Darth Vader with long hair, the Blakwidow cowgirl wearing the black hat. That badass rasslin' beauty in the blue bathing suit.

I was the Goliath to my Montreal opponent's David. My country was the best and I had my big ass flag along with the gold around my waist as proof of the wrestling pudding. I jumped up on the ring and proudly waved Old Glory. It was just as I hoped. The fans were reacting as if I were giving them the middle finger salute instead of the red, white, and blue. This was great!

The ring was getting a little crowded what with the announcer, the referee, and some bald, old guy with a mike. By the time I was done charging and stalking about the ring, the ref had all but dived to the canvas to avoid getting pasted in the head with my flag. Meanwhile the announcer was cautiously standing out of the way in the corner trying to put on a brave face, even though he was basically cowering. Luckily for the old guy, he had to interview the Blakwidow, so he was pretty much safe. At least for the moment.

Now I'm not the sort of woman who really thinks much about what I'm going to say before interviews. My personal preference is to kind of hash out a general framework and then just kind of run with it. So when Jacques told me to "be myself" I was all for it.

"Amanda. You eez da New England champion. Amanda. Amanda . . . eez dat da belt?" the old guy asked. His Quebec accent was pretty thick but I could more or less understand him.

Good, I thought. He's asking a leading question to give the fans information about me and the match. "This is the belt! This is the belt! U-S-A! U-S-A!" I'm not usually the nationalistic type, but hey, I was putting on a show for our little northern cousins. I ripped the title from around my waist and waved it over my head. Hmm . . . he backed away from me a bit. (I wonder if the old boy realized that I was being careful not to hit him. Probably not.)

My only real concern was that monsieur here was being kind of stingy with the mike. So I yelled to make up the dif-ference. But when I reached out and tried to position the microphone closer, he pulled it away. I wonder if Eduardo Carpentier (for that's who the old guy was) thought I was going to grab the mike in classic heel style. The way he was acting I probably would have done just that if my hands weren't already full.

INTRODUCTION

"As I know you are from Killer Kowalski's wrestling school," he said. Sure, his English was a little on the creative side, but it was damn sure better than my non-existent French. If I have one big regret about growing up a mom-and-apple-pie American, it is that English is my only language. Well, I took some Latin and ancient Greek in college but that hardly counts. *Erat hoc mihi dolendum.* Truly. I wonder how many of the fans out there had a clue what I was saying?

"That's right. Killer Kowalski's wrestling school. The same guy who beat you in this very arena, Carpentier. Just like I'm going to beat Canada Girl tonight. Hey, I've got a little song for you. QUAbec sucks!" (I'm told that people from Montreal hate it when you say QUAbec.)

I only got out one "QUAbec sucks," before Carpentier pulled away the mike. Damn. I was hoping to get out at least five of them and maybe even try to get the audience to sing along. I believe this had the potential to be a truly special moment, one I would look back on when I was a toothless old woman in my rocking chair. I'd cackle like an old witch for no apparent reason and the nurses would quickly sedate me. But I'd have my truly-special-moment-number-fourteen.

My opponent made her entrance to a scattered but reasonable round of applause. It is always easier to make the people hate you as opposed to love you . . . well, at least this is generally the case for your humble narrator. But more about wrestling theory later on. On to the match!

I had been out in the ring for about ten minutes but it wasn't time to kick ass yet. After all, the match itself is really only the icing on the cake. All of this crazy stuff that falls under the rubric of "pre-match festivities" is the spectacle that people really throw down their money to see. Otherwise someone might actually care about the Greco-Roman stuff down the road at the junior high school. No disrespect intended, boys, but I have to call it like I see it.

The referee frisked Canada Girl* to make sure she didn't have any concealed weapons. She didn't. (Wow, what a surprise.) Then it was my turn. Naturally I jumped up and sat on the top rope while the referee ran his hands over my boots.

"Don't touch me above my boots!" I screamed. We couldn't have the zebras taking liberties or getting fresh. A chant came up from the crowd, "She's a crack whore! She's a crack whore!" I complained to the referee, who just threw up his hands in disgust. The chant continued, and they soon threw in some rather artistic clapping. Naturally, I was flattered. The time to actually begin the match was clearly at hand.

We locked up and I gave her a hip toss. I took the time to strike a couple of poses for the crowd while Canada Babe got back to her feet. We locked up and down she went again, courtesy of a nasty arm drag. More posing. A third lock-up and this time C.G. got a body slam for her efforts. The crowd was really coming along beautifully. All I had to do was hold up my hands or make a gesture, and the people would erupt with all sorts of sweet profanity that I'm way too much of a

---

*My opponent has asked that I don't mention her name in print, so for the purposes of this book I'll refer to her as Canada Girl (or some variation).

lady to repeat outside of a wrestling locker room.

My victim slowly climbed to her feet. Now the crowd chanted, "We love Canada Girl!" The fans understand the story behind these confrontations of good and evil, so they pretty much knew what was coming. There is a certain enjoyment to a form of entertainment where you know the formula behind the story. Opera, Greek theater, professional wrestling . . . all have certain forms and patterns that the aficionados of each come to expect and appreciate. And one of those patterns is where the babyface eventually outwrestles the heel.

We locked up a fourth time and she gave me a hip toss. I got up fast and caught an arm drag for my efforts. Babe "helped" me up only to slam me. The same three moves I did to her, but all fast from one lock-up. Ouch. I bailed out of the ring and slowed things down.

"Shut up you bunch of faux French frogs! Yeah, well same to you, Pierre!" I bitched at the people a little while I walked around the ring. Canada Girl patiently waited for me in usual babyface fashion.

I had picked up a new move about a week ago at wrestling school and wanted to try it out. So I got back up on the apron, grabbed a handful of Babe's hair, but she punched me twice in the guts. This forced me to grab the top rope so I wouldn't fall off the apron. She grabbed onto the ropes. I yelled, "No! No!" When the moment was right I mumbled, "Now." C.G. jerked on the rope and I came up over the top, ass over elbows, and ended up in the ring flat on my back. This is called going in "the hard way." Admittedly it isn't a

Yeah, Baby!
Victory is the
best revenge
D.J. VON WYC

particularly spectacular maneuver, but it was the first time I had tried it outside of school and it worked! The audience liked it. I know because the fans laughed at me, just as I hoped they would.

She put me in a headlock, quickly worked to a hammerlock, and then around to a headlock again. I decided it was time to get in a little offense of my own and end my opponent's tribute to Ric Flair. So I shot Canada Girl off into the ropes, then slammed her down onto the mat by her blonde hair.

I threw Babe into the ropes and leveled her with a big clothesline. Then I grabbed her by the hair and lifted her straight up about four feet. That had to hurt. Next a few knees to the low back. Finally I tossed Canada Girl into the corner by her throat and laid in some loud, stinging chops to what passed for her bosoms. I had pretty much taken control of the match, and I was hearing it from the crowd. Boy, they sure were pissed off. A pity I couldn't understand most of what they were saying. In any case, it was time for Canada Babe to have a little hope spot.

"Russian leg sweep spot," I whispered. We had done this one in basically all of our matches in the past. Naturally, we shamelessly ripped it off from Val Venis.

"OK," she said. I shot Babe out of the corner and threw her into the opposite turnbuckle. Hard. She staggered out of the corner and I did it again. I grabbed Canada Girl's arm to send her in yet a third time, but she grabbed my arm, twisted it, and put us both on our backs with a quick side Russian leg sweep.

"Babe! Babe! Babe!" the people shouted. They were putty in our hands. We brought them up, but now it was time to quickly take them back down. I got up and gave her a couple of kicks and an elbow drop. After all, I had been beating on her all of this time, so logically one leg sweep wasn't going to change the momentum of the match.

"Amanda sucks!" the fans howled. Hey, at least they knew my name.

"Courtesy to speak English you bunch of goat-barking frogs!" I screamed back. Now I may not be the choicest bit of crumpet in wrestling, but pound for pound I'll bet that Amanda Storm is one of the loudest white women you'll ever see in a wrestling show.

I picked Babe up like a sack of potatoes and hung her upside down in the corner. I once saw an old black-and-white match of Walter Kowalski doing this in Montreal to, you guessed it, Mr. Carpentier. Like Walter, I pounded on my opponent's face until the zebra counted me out of the corner.

"Let's go, Babe!" the crowd yelled. Time to give the crowd a little more to cheer about. I got Babe on the ropes, gave her another one of my patented "Amanda Chops," shot her off, and bent over like I was going to give her a backdrop. But she surprised me with a sunset flip.

I kicked out quickly and got back on her. We went back and forth for about half a minute. Then she blocked my haymaker and punched me once, twice, three times. I was shifting the momentum of the match a little more in her favor. We had the fans hooked and I wanted to give them plenty of reason to root for the hometown hero before we went to our finish. But not too much. I wanted the timing to be perfect. So I raked Canada Girl's eyes and staggered her with an uppercut that sent her reeling into the ropes.

"Crazy woman!"

"Go, Babe!"

"Amanda sucks!"

I got back on top of Canada Girl and indulged myself a little. Amanda choked Babe on the middle rope, stood on her back, and yanked on the middle rope. I have a nice bag of tricks and shortcuts that I learned from Walter Kowalski, and this night I used lots of them for the amusement of my Canadian fans.

INTRODUCTION

Finally I shot her off the ropes and got my face planted firmly into the mat for my efforts. She pinned me but I kicked out on two. Then Babe threw me over the top rope, though only barely. I crawled back up on the ring apron and there came Babe running straight at me. I jumped up, and she baseball slid between my legs and out of the ring. Then she grabbed me by the ankles and yanked. Down went poor Amanda. I didn't exactly enjoy the sensation of my face bouncing off the side of the ring, but you have to expect these things in our business.

Babe shot me toward the crowd but I reversed her and she smacked into the barrier. Hard. Good thing no one was standing directly behind it. If they had, Jacques probably would have killed both of us. I dropped an elbow on Canada Girl as she laid prone on the floor. I picked up the hometown heroine and slammed her into the side of the ring. Then I dumped my opponent on the apron and drove my forearm into her throat. Ah, it was good to be back in the saddle! I made a long trip around the ring and basked in the adulation of the unwashed masses.

"USA sucks!" was their chant of the moment — at least the parts that weren't in French. That and something about me having herpes. The bastards.

"Yeah, well so do you, Pierre!"

Several of the fans showed their class and superior Continental breeding by tossing paper cups and candy wrappers in my general direction. I knew it was clearly time to get back in the ring when someone bounced a Pepsi can off the back of my skull. One syphilitic turd even reached out and grabbed me by the shoulder. A good thing for this idiot that Amanda Storm is a *professional* wrestler. Every fiber of my being (or at least my left deltoid) screamed, "Break his hand! Break it! Break it! Break it!" Instead I took a step back and screamed, "Take your filthy hands off me you QUAbec scum!" At least in the ring I only had to face one opponent and I'd present a moving target to my fans.

I threw Canada Girl around a little more, then gave her a sidewalk slam and went for the pin. Nope, she kicked out on two. I shot Babe in for another sidewalk, but she caught my neck with her legs and flipped me. She banged her hands on the mat and screamed like a girl. This meant Canada Babe was firing up for her big, hometown heroine comeback. Things were starting to look bad for the good old U S of A. Clearly the momentum had shifted entirely over to *fleur-de-lys* girl and the people responded. The fans knew that the end was nigh.

She hit me with a leg drop, shot me into the corner, and gave me a monkey flip. A quick scoop slam, then she climbed the ropes for a missile drop kick. Babe went for a pin. I kicked out. A spinning heel kick next. Yet another slam. Geez, this was starting to get a little old.

"Jesus Christ, go home already," I said as I lay prone in the middle of the ring broken and beaten. She was taking a little long with her comeback and I could hear that we were beginning to lose the fans. Babyface comebacks are exciting stuff but too much of a good thing can spoil the whole game. Clearly it was time to go home. Babe made that Chris Benoit throat cutting motion and mounted the ropes yet again. I'd bet horseshoes to hatpins that Canada Girl had a flying head-butt in mind. Am I a genius or what? Fortunately little Amanda had a plan.

This was not my first match with Babe, so I knew she liked to live on the ropes. I had lost to her once before, but this time I had every intention of hoisting C.G. with her own petard. I was hurt, but not nearly as badly as I was letting on. My plan was when Babe launched herself off that top rope, she'd be kissing the cold, hard mat instead of my poor, abused carcass. (At least that was what I planned on telling the mark mags.)

Smile when you raise my hand next time, Zebraboy

D.J. VON WYC

But I didn't get a chance to put my plan into action. Canada Girl was just getting her footing on the top rope when a straw-haired midget came out with a blow-up doll. ("Midget" is an appropriate term in professional wrestling. I don't have time for any stinking political correctness.) The kicker was that the doll had a blonde wig just like my bleach-blonde opponent. Naturally I was having a devil of a time not breaking into torrents of laughter. It was just this sort of silliness that keeps wrestling from resembling a real sport (and makes it more interesting).

Apparently the midget had some sort of heat going with Canada Girl. He seemed hell-bent on distracting her, but I was pretty sure that this whole farce wasn't for Amanda Storm's benefit. As I understand, C.G. and he had wrestled some matches before I came along. I've never been the sort of girl to let opportunity pass her by, so I wandered over to the corner and gave Babe a nasty punch in the guts. Then I flung her off the top rope into the middle of the ring. Ouch. I didn't want any chance of a kickout so up Canada Girl went for a powerbomb, and then I pressed those narrow Canadian shoulders to the mat for that sweet one - two - three!

Yee haw! I grabbed my flag and skipped around the center of the ring celebrating yet another clean victory. The Canadian referee had proven himself amazingly annoying and biased towards the hometown favorite. Now I didn't begrudge the frog fans for cheering on their girl from Montreal, but I do expect a certain degree of impartiality from the zebra. It was way past the last straw when he started arguing with the midget instead of raising Amanda Storm's hand in victory like a good little referee.

So I spun zebraboy around, kicked him in the guts, then gave him a move that was a bizarre cross between a vertical suplex and a powerslam. I had originally planned on a snap suplex, but the old boy went up like the proverbial sack of potatoes. So I did what I could to keep from dropping the referee on his head, while entertaining the fans at the same time. Of course I beat him with my flag. (I do fancy myself an artist, after all.)

Canada Girl was still writhing around in the middle of the ring, so I gave her a quick boot to the belly and jumped out of the ring. The time was at hand for the truly fun part of the match — exchanging my final "pleasantries" with the audience. And boy were they pissed.

I wandered by the media table. "Scribble that in your notebooks!" I sneered. I could hear Jacques's voice in my head telling me to say that line to the press boys. I toyed with the idea of jumping up on the media tables and doing a little dance. After a brief moment of reflection I decided to go with a minimalist approach and just run through my muscle-posing routine while cracking insults.

"Anyone mistake you for a man?" one of the newsmen a couple rows back in the media section shouted. Brave boy. God, his neck was about as big as my wrist. He was the sort of guy you'd see in *Blue Boy*, except he was small and ugly.

"Nope. How about you, you little faux frog sissy boy?" I cackled as I hit a double biceps shoot. It all goes to show that

BLAKWIDOW

Seneca was right when he wrote, "*Quod sentimus loquamur quod loquimur sentiamus concordet sermo cum vita.*" (Roughly, "Let us say what we feel; let us feel what we say: may our speech agree with our lives, baby.") God I love my job. . . .

CHAPTER ONE

THE ROCKING CHAIR TEST

"And in this corner at 275 pounds, Killer Kowalski," the announcer intoned and before he could finish "Kowalski" the people were hurling boo's and whistles at the huge, rather impassive-looking man leaning against the ropes near the corner. He absolutely towered over his opponent, whose name I don't remember. He was just another bland babyface who was a foil for Killer's wrestling antics.

"That goddamn Kowalski," my grandfather said, gesturing at the television. "He was a right bastard but what a wrestler!"

My granddad had a huge collection of old black-and-white wrestling matches that he had transferred from tape onto VHS. He also had a lot of newer material that he recorded directly off the television. My wrestling training really began at my grandfather's knee. I would sit at his feet and huddle up against the air conditioner while we watched his tapes and he did his own color commentary. Granddad was very enthusiastic about wrestling and he made staying indoors on those blistering Roseville summer days a lot of fun. The only problem was that he had seen most of the matches about a thousand times and he would often get excited and start telling me about things that were going to happen five minutes down the road.

Before my grandfather, wrestling wasn't something that really entered into my consciousness. Like most girls I was caught up with Barbie and my Easy Bake oven. But I soon came to appreciate the likes of Pat Patterson, Buddy Rodgers, Andre the Giant, Ivan Putski, Special Delivery Jones, Gorgeous George, and a host of others. One of the first things that I noticed was that the "bad guys" were the most interesting and certainly the most colorful. My grandfather, despite calling them all "right bastards," seemed to agree. It wasn't long before I had caught his enthusiasm and knew what was going to happen five minutes in the future of any given match as well. When he and I watched wrestling, everyone else knew the best thing was to leave us alone.

"Are there women wrestlers too, Grampy?" I asked one day.

"Oh sure, the ladies wrestle, and some of them are right bastards!" he said laughing.

"Really? How come you don't have any women wrestlers on tape?"

"That's a good question, Alex. We'll have to do something about that!"

I don't know where he got it and I didn't think to ask but I was soon treated to the likes of Moolah, June Byers, and Vivian Vachon, who was my favorite and definitely a "right bastard." I soon proclaimed that I too wanted to become a girl wrestler and styled myself as Amanda Vachon. My grandfather encouraged me, though in retrospect I think that he was just going along with something that he thought would pan out to be a child's short-lived fantasy. My parents, on the other hand, flipped. They absolutely forbade me to watch any more professional wrestling. At first I was devastated, but within a month I went back to my Barbie and Easy Bake oven and all was right with the world again. But despite my parents' best efforts, wrestling never went away entirely. My grandfather secretly dubbed me tapes of matches and we still talked about wrestling when we got the chance. And as I got a bit older and my parents weren't in a position to monitor my television habits, I started watching WWF *Superstars* and other such fare.

Unfortunately, the world at the time didn't really support the idea of women in contact sports. Like most people, I got caught up in the day-to-day grind of living, and wrestling soon became a pipe dream and a "what if." Instead my interests in athletics were channeled towards softball and field hockey, and away from wrestling. I did look into training for amateur wrestling in high school but was essentially told by the coach to "go away." So I played first base, learned what I could about amateur wrestling from books and practiced on my dog. (Ever try to put a grapevine on a German Shepherd?

It is harder than you'd think. Especially when there is no referee to give him the five count when he bites.)

Eventually I went to state college in California where I majored in English and graduated *summa cum laude*. I enjoyed college and if I had been independently wealthy I probably would have immersed myself in the world of academics and never come out. I very much enjoy reading books on a wide range of subjects, and often would go to the library and just wander around in the stacks, often picking out a book at random. So majoring in English seemed the logical choice. A number of people questioned my choice of majors, arguing that I wouldn't be able to make money and that I should choose something more technical or perhaps a trade like

Spring dawns in Wiccan Park
D.J. VON WYC

nursing. However, my philosophy at the time was that I would study what I enjoyed and then try to figure out a way to make money at it. In retrospect I'm glad because without knowing it at the time, I was preparing myself to write this book!

I worked a number of different jobs in college. I took a job as a waitress, held any number of different office jobs, was a crossing guard for about two weeks, a desk attendant at a gym, and a doorwoman at a lesbian bar. But once I graduated from college I landed a "real" job as a technical writer, which was basically taking computer programmer jargon and turning it into language regular people could understand for software manuals.

When I was in college I tried to balance studying what I enjoyed with the post-college reality that was always on the horizon like an angry green storm cloud. I majored in English but I also did a short internship at a small software house in Sacramento. After I graduated they offered me a full-time position. I was working in cubicle hell for about three months when I had a conversation with my grandfather that changed my life. I was unhappy and bored out of my mind but I was making fantastic money. Everyone who said that I shouldn't have majored in English was very happy for me.

Grampy was in a nursing home and we all knew that we could lose him at any time. I was visiting him as often as I could, about three or four times a week. I lived about an hour away but I figured that with his declining health, I needed to make the time because I'd have some serious regrets otherwise. Needless to say, we talked a lot about wrestling and those "right bastards." And I talked about how I hated my job but liked the money. My grandfather was quiet for a moment. He was obviously visiting the hazy world of his past.

"Alexandra, let me tell you about the rocking chair test," he said quietly. I nodded. The seriousness in his voice made it seem inappropriate somehow for me to speak.

"No matter how much money you make or what you do in life, everyone ends up in the same boat when the game is over." He looked significantly at the tubes that were hooked all over his body and at the medical machinery that was keeping him alive.

His point was not lost on me.

"The key to a successful life is to do the things that will make you happy or at least do your damnedest to try. If you like writing, then write. If you like fixing cars, then do that. The trick is to live your life so that when you are old and used up like me you won't have any regrets. You have a lot of time to just sit and think towards the end, a lot of time to dwell on the good times, the bad, and what might have been. I call it the Rocking Chair Test. If you have more good times than bad and more happiness than regrets, then you pass. If not, well, there is no second try."

I was going to point out the doctrine of Reincarnation but thought the better of it.

"So Alex, I don't know what you want to do with your life and you're young so you have time, but figure out what you want and remember the Rocking Chair Test."

"Gramps, you remember how we used to watch wrestling together?"

"Yes, hon," he said smiling. "We had wonderful times. You were so cute when you'd do Chief Jay Strongbow's little dance and say you were a "right bastard.""

"Well, I still want to be a professional wrestler."

"Then become a wrestler and you'll make me proud."

At that point the conversation ended and we both cried like babies. He passed away a few months later, just before my first professional match. Maybe someday my singlet will have a rocking chair sewn on the front in memory of my Grampy, who was the first person who honestly told me to damn the torpedoes and follow my dreams.

CHAPTER TWO

"SORRY, WE AREN'T SET UP FOR GIRLS"

STORMDATE: April, 1998.

"I can train you as a valet for $5,000."

"That's a lot of money." I stifled an urge to respond with something like, "Screw you, scumbag." But if I have learned one thing in my 30-something years on planet Earth, it is to go with my second or even third impulse. The bridge you burn today might be the one you need to cross tomorrow.

"If you want the best then you have to pay for it." I could hear the smirk in his voice.

"Um, could you suggest someone who could train me to wrestle?" I asked the cigarette-coated voice from Hayward, California.

Pregnant pause.

"Well, we are the premier school on the West Coast."

"Well, not if you are a woman who wants to be a wrestler."

Pregnant pause number two.

"Well, we're not set up for that. But I can train you to be a first-class valet for $5,000."

"OK, thank you, goodbye," I said quickly. I didn't slam the phone. No point in taking out my frustration on poor, defenseless technology.

Silly girl. I figured that all I would have to do is open my local yellow pages, make a couple of phone calls and I'd be in like Flynn. Nothing simpler.

Think again. Another phone call and another place that "wasn't set up for girls." So there was nothing to do but cross the "premier school on the West Coast" off my list and try again. I didn't realize it at the time, but my training as a wrestler had already begun.

Lesson da first: Never give up. Even if everyone and everything is against you. *Especially* if everyone and everything is against you. My original plan was to stay in California, preferably northern California, and continue to work as a technical writer by day while I trained as a wrestler by night. The only problem with my "Grand Plan" was that I had crossed off all of the schools on my list. My main concern had been whether or not the school would be any good. It never occurred to me that simply finding a school, *any* school, would be the chief obstacle. That was when a ray of sunshine peeked through the wrestling school fog.

I had sent a letter to a school called Slammers down in

southern California, along with the requisite check for their information packet. Some weeks later, a big manila envelope came back with my name on it! Happy Happy! Joy Joy!

My heart sank as I rifled through the pages. Uh oh. No personal letter. No "Dear Amanda." Not even a "Dear Prospective Student." Just a yellow booklet outlining their training program and the details of how tough it was to become a successful professional wrestler. Beside the requisite pictures of students doing unpleasant things to each other, I noticed a paragraph circled in red. The gist of it was basically something like, "We aren't set up for girls." At least they were kind enough to provide an address for Moolah's school, which I learned trains female wrestlers. I fired off a letter the same day. To this day, I have never received a reply. So much for lightning. At least this time around.

Great Caesar's Ghost, it was all so frustrating! This difficulty in finding a wrestling school was threatening to become a very dangerous time for me, or at least for my goals. I really hate to admit this, but I have had a bit of a problem with my weight in the past. In fact, when I graduated from college in 1996 I had achieved an all-time high of 242 pounds. Kind of on the light side for an NFL defensive lineman, but a tad on the repulsively titanic side for a 5' 7" woman.

I have always been an active person though, so I was in surprisingly good shape even as Leviathan Girl. For example, I lifted weights all through college. After two hours of Chaucer or Shakespeare, I often found solace blasting iron or playing racquetball for an hour or so. On the other hand, I didn't find the treadmill or exercise bike overly diverting, and it showed.

I didn't know it at the time, but there certainly is a precedent for incredibly obese female wrestlers. I just wasn't going to be one of them. So I ramped up my aerobics. I cut back on the weights and started doing 45-minute sessions on the exercise bike or treadmill five days a week. Plus I got serious about my diet, cut out a lot of the fat, and avoided carbohydrates late at night. I didn't get weird about it, but within a year I trimmed down to 185 pounds. As I type these words I weigh in at 170 pounds and have not gained any of the weight back. I could probably stand to lose 10 more pounds, but hey, you can't have everything!

Like I said before, this was a dangerous time for me. When I get depressed, the easiest road for me to follow is the one that leads directly to the refrigerator. It would have been simple to say to myself, "Well, no one will train me because I'm a woman. Boo hoo! I'm so oppressed," and drown my sorrows with a pint of Ben & Jerry's while ruminating on the nature of Justice or the Form of the Good or some other such nonsense.

Luckily for me I was focused. The only road I followed was the one around Curtis Park in good old Sacramento. Curtis Park is a patch of greenery bounded by a mile-long trail located about four miles south of the capitol. The park attracts all kinds of characters. When my husband was nine years old he stole his father's '54 Ford pick-up and spun donuts from one end of the grass to the other. Good old

Curtis Park. An island of oak, grass, and sycamore in an ocean of homelessness and concrete.

So four days a week I biked over to the park and nodded at the lesbians as I ran laps and they walked their dogs. Still, the reality of Amanda Storm wrestling in a show was a far away star, flickering through the haze of a smoggy Sacramento night. . . .

CHAPTER THREE

"CALL ME WALTER"

STORMDATE: September, 1998.

Almost four months had passed since I had started searching for a wrestling school. I had continued looking in the back of wrestling magazines, contacting indie federations on the 'Net, and so forth. I had gotten a few nibbles and a couple of bites, but nothing real promising had come my way yet. If I was learning one valuable lesson from my search it was this: wrestling is full of grifters, con artists, and people out to steal everyone else's candy.

One day I came back from a run in Curtis Park. I rode my bike the seven miles or so to the park, ran three miles, and then rode back. I was busy stretching when my hubby yelled, "You have a call from some guy named Walter, hon."

"Hello?" I had no idea who this person was on the other end of the phone.

"This is Walter Kowalski. Is this Amanda?"

"Yes. Hello." Who the hell was Walter Kowalski? I decided to play along like I knew him just in case I was supposed to know him. (Tell me that you haven't done the same thing with people.)

"I got your letter about the wrestling school," the gruff voice informed me.

"Wonderful! So you train women?" I was starting to get a clue.

"Yes. Men and women are both welcome."

"So you train women to wrestle, not just manage?" I asked. Now I knew who it was: "Killer" Kowalski, who my grandfather and I had watched for so many years. He now ran a wrestling school on the East Coast.

"We treat everyone the same. I trained Chyna and I'm always happy to have more girls at my school. I won't treat you any different than the guys. I don't train women wrestlers, I train wrestlers."

Wow. This was sounding way too good to be true.

"I'd like to come out and meet you, and see what New England is like, Mr. Kowalski. This is a big step for me but I'm very serious about becoming a wrestler."

"I see." He paused for a second. "I will be at a show on the 19th in New Hampshire and another down in Connecticut on the 20th. Several of my students will be in both shows. Feel free to come and watch, and please introduce yourself."

Damn! It was sounding like I had hit the jackpot. I could

Generations: Master and apprentice
D.J. VON WYC

hardly contain my excitement as I scribbled down the directions to the shows from the Boston airport. He was kind enough to also recommend a couple of inexpensive motels in the area as well as places to eat.

"Thank you. I will definitely be at both shows, Mr. Kowalski."

"Call me Walter."

I got off the phone with Mr. Kowalski and booked my flight, hotel, and all the rest. You had better believe that I endured more than a couple of sleepless nights waiting for the start of my wrestling trip. So I threw myself into my workouts and counted down the days. It was pretty funny. I had a calendar in the bathroom with the Big Day circled in red with big stars and smiley faces. Each night I would cross a day off the calendar like a little kid waiting for Christmas. That is exactly how I felt. I was filled with an exuberance that we usually experience only as children, when each day is fresh and the world is young. Finally that big day circled in red with big stars and smiley faces had arrived!

I endured the seven-hour plane ride from Sacramento to Boston, though I have to admit the processed chicken patty wasn't too bad. Mostly I looked out the window a lot when the pilot would run through his "and now we are over" speeches but all I could ever see were the tops of the clouds. The next day I was driving my rented Neon to Goshen, New Hampshire with a growing sense of trepidation. What if Walter didn't like me? What if I couldn't find the show? What if I was hit by a two-mile-wide hunk from one of the rings of Saturn? What if . . . what if . . . what if?

I found the high school fairly easily. I didn't know it at the time but I used what has become my standard method of finding my way to shows. Promoters and bookers, God love 'em, are very busy people and sometimes the directions they e-mail the wrestlers are a little on the garbled side or just plain wrong. Often they haven't been to the town in question either, so they don't really have any more of an idea where the show is than anyone else does. Plus, they have a million other things to worry about besides little Amanda Storm.

"CALL ME WALTER"

So this is the drill: I find the town and stop at the nearest convenience store. By this time my bladder is invariably ready to burst because I'm a diet cola fiend. I use the bathroom or go behind their dumpster if it "isn't open to the public." Then I come back inside and buy something so I won't seem like a freeloader and ask, "Where is the high school?" They give me directions and from there I just look for the ring truck. Once I find that big white Budget or Ryder I know that I have arrived.

People were busy putting the ring together, setting up chairs and barriers, organizing the merchandise table, and in general doing all of the big and little things that go into putting on an "independent" wrestling show. So I just walked in unnoticed and sat and watched everything that was going on. I seriously doubt that anyone who knows Amanda Storm now would have recognized the timid girl with raven tresses huddled up all alone on the corner of the bleachers in her oversized San Francisco sweatshirt and gray leggings. (By coincidence I just happen to be wearing that very sweat shirt as I type these words almost two years later.)

I was daydreaming as I watched an older woman, who turned out to be the promoter's wife, organizing a stack of DX foam hands when I was gently interrupted by a male voice.

"Excuse me, Miss. Do you know where the dressing room is, please?" He had just a hint of a southern drawl. I looked up and who was it but Jeff Jarrett standing there holding his suitcases, wearing a baseball cap and some dark, tortoise-shell sunglasses. He set his bags down, took off his glasses, and smiled at me.

"Um, no, Sir, I don't. I'm just here to talk to someone about wrestling school."

"Oh! That's great! May I?" Jeff asked, gesturing that he wanted to sit down beside me.

"Sure! I'm Amanda," I said, smiling. Wow. He was wearing my favorite, Old Spice. (Or maybe I'm just remembering it that way because he was so nice when I was feeling a little scared and vulnerable. I don't know.)

"Nice to meet you, Amanda. I'm Jeff. If you don't mind my asking, why do you want to become a wrestler?"

"Well, I like sports and I like performing in theater and I see wrestling as a way to do both at the same time."

"I see," Jeff said, nodding. He paused for a second and looked at me. "I'm sure you'll do great."

"Thank-you-if-you-don't-mind-my-asking-why-did-you-become-a-wrestler-and-if-you-could-give-someone-new-one-important-piece-of-advice-what-would-it-be?" That was how I was talking. I figured that someone like me doesn't get to sit and chew the fat every day with someone like Jeff, so I wanted to ask him my questions before he could make his inevitable escape.

"It was something that I have wanted to do for a long time," he said, looking remote and somewhat wistful. "Anyone that gets into this business gives up a lot, but it gets in your blood. It really does."

I nodded and made little agreeing noises. (These are cues we women use, mainly with each other, to say, "Please continue talking. I'm affirming what you say and want you to keep going." I read that in one of those "Venus and Mars" type of articles that tend to be in vogue with women's magazines these days.) Jeff hunched over, widened his legs a bit, and clasped his hands together. This is the male signal for, "We're just a couple of good old boys shooting the shit and having a good talk." I was pleased to see that he was comfortable talking to me. For some reason I've always connected well with men, which has served me well as a wrestler for obvious reasons.

"It is very easy to become discouraged in wrestling because there are a lot of dishonest people. There are promoters who will stiff you on your pay or cancel shows at the last minute, and other wrestlers who will run you down behind your back while putting you over to your face. This is a very political business. The best way to get along is to always be very honest with people and don't believe things unless you see them with your own eyes or hear them with your own ears. Just realize that you'll have good times and lean times, setbacks and injuries. Take the good with the bad, stay true to yourself, and you'll do just fine."

A guy in his late 40s with glasses, wearing jeans and a white turtleneck sweater wandered over and politely gestured in Jeff's direction. "Uh, Jeff, could I talk to you for a second?" he asked.

"Sure, be right there. Listen, it was very nice meeting you, Amanda, and good luck with wrestling school. I'm sure we'll get a chance to talk again someday. I hope you enjoy the show."

"Thank you very much, Jeff." I stood up and watched as he picked up his bags and walked away with the promoter, whose name was Freddie. I watched them leave through the curtain, which was blue instead of black. Wow, all that and brains too.

I watched as the undercard wrestlers began to trickle in and the crew finished with the ring and began setting up the chairs. Finally, after about a half hour they started letting in the fans. Freddie happened to notice me still camping in the bleachers and waved me over.

"Come on. I want to introduce you to someone," he said.

I followed Freddie through the blue curtain into the back.

The calm before the storm
D.J. VON WYC

Once we figured out where the girls' locker room was located, he yelled in to make sure that "everyone was decent" and introduced me to Brandi Alexander. She was sitting on a bench lacing up her boots. We had a short conversation about how, yes, I wanted to become a wrestler. I was terrified of saying the wrong thing of course, but I did a pretty good job of acting cool but respectful. The thing that struck me about Brandi was that she and I were about the same height. I could tell that Brandi was mentally preparing herself for her match so I didn't want to take up too much of her time. So I thanked her for seeing me and made my way back to the auditorium. When I left, Brandi was in her costume pacing back and forth in the shower. A few months later, once I was performing in shows, I would pace in showers all over New England myself.

Later on I got to see Brandi Alexander in the ring. I enjoyed their match and the people were definitely into the action, cheering for the babyface Alexander. I especially liked a move that Brandi did where she hopped up onto the second rope and jumped off, catching her opponent with a cross-body. (I've seen used that move myself on those rare occasions where I am a babyface.) Brandi lost the match when her heel foe cold cocked her with a concealed weapon, but the ever vigilant "Commissioner" Kowalski reversed the decision, much to the delight of the fans.

The show stealer was of course Jeff Jarrett against my future teacher, Mike Hollow. They had a great back-and-forth technical match that was vintage Hollow. In his own words,

Mike is a "pretty boring guy." What he means is that he does a lot of basic stuff, but he puts moves together and paces his matches in such a way that gets people excited. Needless to say, he had a very good opponent to work with in Jeff Jarrett. You don't really get to see how spectacular someone like Jeff is by watching him on those short television matches. Mike Hollow vs. Jeff Jarrett was a match that I was thrilled to see in person. I kick myself to this day that I didn't think to bring a camera.

So up to this point I had met everyone in the world but the man I flew, drove, and walked 3,600 miles to see, which was Mr. Kowalski. I saw him from a distance a couple of times before the show began but for some reason I got a case of the shy's and didn't go up and introduce myself. Pretty smart, huh? Ah well, the beautiful thing about life is that we always have tomorrow to repeat the mistakes of today.

The next day found me in the beautiful town of Wallingford, Connecticut at — believe it or not — a used car dealership. I sure was getting a taste of probably what is the hardest thing about being a professional wrestler — the travel. I now put a thousand wrestling-related miles a week on my car, which doesn't include the miles I log when I am renting out my ring to someone. But I digress as usual. . . .

Yes, apparently Tony Rumble's National Wrestling Alliance of New England was holding a show outside in the middle of a parking lot. I remember seeing King Kong "Please Call Me Chris" Bundy for the first time. Ironically, the first time I saw him he kind of struck me as a bit of an ass. I say "ironic" because his and my paths have crossed a lot at shows over the past year, and I couldn't have been more wrong. Chris is a super nice guy.

Anyway, he was complaining about how cold it was outside and if I had to wear that black singlet like he did on a fall day in New England, I would have complained too. This California girl was wearing a sweatshirt and a sweater and I was still shivering. Ah, the sacrifices we make when we pursue the things we love. The important thing was that Walter was at the show so I had a second chance to meet him. He was sitting inside the showroom at a table selling autographed pictures of himself to the kids and the old timers, who would reminisce about Yukon Eric's missing ear or how they saw him at the Garden in '68 and so on. Mr. Kowalski would smile and say a few quiet words in reply. He was clearly enjoying himself, so I stood back and fended off the herd of sharks in polyester who kept trying to sell me an SUV while I waited. And oh boy, I was terrified. I didn't really know that much about the Killer Kowalski legend or the man himself, but I definitely wanted to go to his wrestling school. I had seen a number of his students in action and I could tell that this was the place for me. After all, he trained Chyna and she went from selling pagers and having the nickname "Beeper Whore" among her wrestling friends to who she is today.

Finally my big moment came. I felt just like I so often did in speech class. You know that feeling? There was nothing to do but screw up my courage, walk up to that table, and introduce myself.

"Hello, Mr. Kowalski, I'm Amanda, the one who called

you from California about wrestling school."

Boy, did he ever look surprised. He broke into a big smile and shook me by the hand. I use the British colloquialism advisedly. Mr. Kowalski is a huge man and he has basketball player hands. He has to be at least 6′ 7″. That is big by any standard but in "his day" (as he likes to call it) he was practically a giant.

"I thought someone was working me!" he said with a gruff laugh. "I thought there was no way some woman from California was going to come all the way out here to talk to me about wrestling school. But here you are!" He gave me his business card, which I still carry around in my wallet. (Actually I have several different versions of his card, one of which has his picture on the front. Later on I started doing the same thing with my own business card.)

"Yes, here I am. I am very interested in your school, Mr. Kowalski." I wasn't quite sure what he meant by "working me" but I was relieved to find that he turned out to be a very nice man. He told me some more about his school and I bought an autographed picture from him for my grandfather. Much to my embarrassment I only had a 20 and he didn't have any change. The polyester sharks couldn't help me unless I bought an suv, so I had to go into the snack bar and come back with his change.

"I bet you thought that I was going to disappear and stiff you on that picture," I said smiling when I came back and paid him.

"I did, but I decided to just beat you up the first day of

class," he replied casually, holding up a huge hand in a menacing claw-like gesture.

I laughed and reflected on the myriad advantages of being reasonably honest as women go. "Thank you, Mr. Kowalski. I'd like to start on December 21st and get in a few days before you close for the holidays. If that is OK."

"That's fine. Take care and thank you. And call me *Walter*."

"Yes, Sir, Mr. Kowalski, er, Walter."

CHAPTER FOUR

YOU'LL MAKE ME A STAR?

STORMDATE: April–November, 1998.

I already had a small but growing fan base even though I was still living in Sacramento. I had started a Web site back in April, 1998, where I billed myself as "The Black Widow," who "dissembled men the way a curious child might a pocket watch." I chose a spider motif because I have always been fascinated by spiders and loved them dearly. I had a pet Tarantula I named Caligula, after the allegedly insane Roman emperor. I also routinely rescued little collectives of black widows from under my steps and released them down by the river where they could find some measure of safety, at least from the exterminator.

I didn't know anything about building a Web site and started out small, slowly adding what I could as I learned more about how to construct a basic site, which is a process that continues to this day. One thing I noticed early on was that a site like mine lives or dies by its pictures and I didn't have any. So Donald and I went to a local graveyard where we often went to do our morning power walk and took some. I decked myself out in a black leather corset and accessories that I bought at Stormy Leather in San Francisco, some black tights, and my Harley boots. A little lipstick and I was ready.

I posed in front of a couple of interesting-looking mausoleums while Donald snapped away with his 35mm. I felt a little strange and perhaps slightly self-conscious as I flexed my biceps or hit a pose with my handcuffs while the morning walkers stared as they walked by. A small part of me wondered if perhaps I was being disrespectful in a sacred place. I've given a lot of thought to this because I have always been fascinated by graveyards and drawn to quiet, forgotten places. I was the sort of girl who read once in a book that a person can look out from between the ears of a dog in a graveyard and see ghosts. Within a week I had borrowed my neighbor's dog so I could try.

Anyway, I don't think that I was being disrespectful and even if some of the dead thought that I was, I'm sure the overall opinion was divided. A graveyard, among other things, is a place of remembrance for those who would otherwise be completely forgotten. When I am dead, if some whacked-out chick in a leather bondage outfit wants to dance on my grave while her husband snaps promotional pictures for her wrestling Web site, then as far as I'm concerned more power to them both. If such a thing is possible, I'll claw my

Beware the Tarantulas
D.J. VON WYC

way up out of the earth, knock the grave mold and worms out of my empty skull, and proceed to offer them advice on all aspects of the wrestling business.

We had the pictures developed and put the best ones up on the site. I wrote a little narrative to go with them called, "Beware the Tarantulas." The feedback was extremely favorable and soon after I changed my address from a bunch of unreadable alphabet soup to blakwidow.com. (I had to go with the odd spelling because "blackwidow.com" had already been taken.)

The Web site was my first attempt to introduce myself to wrestling fans. I didn't say that I was a wrestler on the site. I just put up the pictures and my writing and hoped that

Princess
Axloaptolcetta of the
Ninth Dynasty lives
again
D.J. VON WYC

people would find what I was doing interesting. Much to my delight they did. I can clearly remember the first time someone e-mailed me, inquiring how much an autographed picture would cost. I was absolutely on Cloud Nine. I didn't actually have pictures for sale because I assumed that people would just download them from the internet, if they were interested at all. It hadn't occurred to me that someone would actually want my autograph *and* my picture. So I made a few phone calls and struck a deal with a local photo company to make some black and white 8 x 10s from pictures Donald had taken of me in the graveyard and amidst some abandoned buildings on the Presidio.

I started selling pictures on my site and later at wrestling shows. Nothing will ever top the thrill of that first picture though. What should I write on it? Should I write just my name? Or maybe some cute saying? I really had no idea but I had a great time thinking about it. Finally I settled upon a wrestling adaptation of a famous quote:

Hey there Frank!

For whom does the bell toll?
It tolls for thee.
I'm coming to get you,
Pin you one-two-three!

Love,
The Blakwidow

Well, Frank, I hope you enjoyed that picture and as far as I'm concerned the first autographed copy of my book will be waiting for you too. I have always felt that a person should remember and do good by people who bring them happiness in life, and that first autograph brought me a lot of pleasure. (The technical term, I would find out later on, is "marking out for yourself.")

Not long after this first picture, Donald and I both thought that I needed a regular name, instead of just going through life as the "Blakwidow." We made a list of names and our friends added their picks, but nothing really stood out.

One day Donald came home from work and proclaimed, "Why don't you just use your real name?"

"Alexandra Whitney? Well, I suppose there is something to be said for the minimalist approach."

"No, your name before we got married. A guy at work

suggested it."

"You talk about wrestling at work?" I was pretty surprised because while Donald was extremely supportive of my getting into wrestling, he definitely wasn't a fan.

"No, one of the contractors spends all of his time surfing the wrestling Web sites and wrestling is all he talks about. He checks your site regularly and it was his idea."

So I became "The Blakwidow" Amanda Storm, which I think was a pretty good idea. Amanda is also my grandmother's name, so I thought my grandfather would get a kick out of it if he were still alive.

All that remained was my quest to find a place to train and I had found a likely school in Kowalski's. The only fly in that particular jar of ointment was that New England was a world away from Sacramento. But bridging the gulf was the I-80, relatively cheap gasoline, and a culture that encourages a certain rootlessness or at least restlessness, certainly in people under 35. So I continued looking for a school in California while simultaneously making preparations to move.

One day as I was walking home from the gym, I noticed a poster proclaiming that professional wrestling was coming to the Memorial Auditorium. Now this was exciting news because I only lived four blocks away! Maybe if I was lucky I could go to the show and get the promoter to notice me. So I threw on a sleeveless dress that showed off my arms, paid my 10 dollars and got a seat near where the wrestlers would be making their entrance. They had a nice crowd and even had Greg Valentine and the Honky Tonk Man as their headliners.

I had a good time watching the matches, though I grew sad as I sat sipping a Diet Coke during intermission and watching the people line up for a Polaroid with either Greg or Honky Tonk. I was almost on the verge of tears because I was having such a good time and it brought back bittersweet memories of how my now departed grandfather had introduced me to wrestling. I was standing near the barrier looking into my drink when something I totally didn't expect happened. I felt someone grab a big handful of my ass!

Normally I am a fairly even-tempered person, but this time I basically came unglued. I turned around and in front of me was a sunburned guy with long, kind of greasy black hair sporting a "Kill them all, let God sort them out" T-shirt. He had a big shit-eating grin on his face and was at least a head taller than me.

"You look like a wrestler, honey," he said, laughing. "Can I have your autograph? You gonna be in the show later?"

"Yeah, here's an autograph for you," I said, laughing back and slamming the knife edge of my hand into his Adam's apple. Then I kicked him in the side of the knee and as he went down, Kill Them All Boy smacked his head on the steel barrier. I jumped on top of him, wrapped my legs around his midsection, and started choking him out with my arms. Normally I'm not this way at all. Normally I'm probably very even-tempered and definitely not prone to violence, but like I said before, I snapped. I think the lesson here is don't harass chicks who want to become wrestlers when they are musing about mortality and their dear departed ancestors. (If you must, at least don't grab their ass.)

Suddenly I felt a dozen rough arms lifting me bodily into the air. I just went limp and hoped they weren't the guy's friends and if they were that they wouldn't beat me up too badly. I did notice that they were all wearing red shirts, so I figured they were probably security like in Star Trek.

The Mercenary guy slowly got up and made a move to come at me when a red-shirted gentleman, who looked suspiciously like Perry Saturn, jumped in his face and yelled, "You got your ass kicked once tonight by a chick. Be smart and get the hell out of here. Now!" No one had to tell him twice. I don't think I've ever seen someone outside of track and field make for the doors as fast as this guy did.

The security guys were escorting me to the doors as well, though they were being fairly nice about it. At least I was walking under my own power and they were all obviously trying not to laugh about the whole situation. Looking back on it, and the fact there wasn't a lawsuit and no one came back with a gun, it was pretty funny, but at the time I was beside myself. This wasn't the kind of attention I was hoping for.

"Can I at least call my husband so I can get a ride? That guy might be out there with a knife or three of his friends or something," I pleaded, on the verge of tears. They let me go once we were out in the foyer. One of them handed me my purse and another gave me back my hair scrunchie that had fallen out in the altercation.

"There's a pay phone right there," the obvious ringleader of the security guys said. "If we leave you here to use it, there aren't going to be any more problems, right?"

"No, sir, no problems and thank you." The leader nodded and motioned for his crew to follow him as he went back into the auditorium. A slightly overweight older guy in a wrestling T-shirt walked up to me while I was fishing around in my purse for a quarter. Oh great, another one.

"Yes?" I said, bristling a little. I was hoping he wasn't a friend of the guy I had just fought with. I had told the security guard there wouldn't be any trouble and I felt very ashamed for making a scene. Looking back on it and knowing what I do now about wrestling, I'll bet that most of the audience thought the whole thing was some sort of work and were surprised that neither of us were in the show later.

"Have you ever thought about going into wrestling?" he asked.

"Yes. Why do you want to know?"

I could see that he was a little nervous.

"My name is Peter and I'm the booker for Sacramento Valley Wrestling. I was thinking that if you could channel some of that aggression into wrestling, you could make a lot of money." I was going to tell him that I'm not normally the violent type, but I could tell that he wanted to keep talking so I just nodded a lot and let him. "We could have you help out behind the scenes with setting up the ring, chairs and stuff like that, which is how everyone starts out. Later on we'll train you to be a valet."

"Really?" My mood was quickly improving.

"Oh yes, and we'll pay you too. We don't expect you to

work for free."

Thus began my short involvement with the Sacramento Valley Wrestling Alliance. I didn't realize it at the time, but the SVWA was basically run by a man who conned whoever he could into fronting money for his next show, which he would promptly lose by booking too many stars, apparently so he could have his picture taken with them.

His staff was mostly people like myself who wanted to "break into the business." Peter took advantage of their enthusiasm and hoped to garner a source of free labor for his little shoestring enterprise. The "pay" turned out to be credit, which would later be deducted from subsequent training. In my case this training never came and as far as I could see none of the other people received any wrestling or valet training either.

I did learn a lot about setting up rings and I got an inkling of how much work went into running a show. But if Peter had been straight with me, I probably would have agreed to help him anyway. I did want to learn about the mechanics of wrestling rings and I enjoyed being a part of the scene. True, he probably got a lot more work out of me by lying and feeding my hopes than if he had been honest. Still, you would think there would be some advantage to building a successful business by fostering trust, loyalty, and goodwill in one's employees?

One day Peter called me aside and asked me to step into his "office," which was a stack of boxes in a storeroom of the auditorium we were playing in that night.

"Did you bring that dominatrix outfit?" Peter asked as he looked over that night's card (which he had scribbled down on the back of a magazine).

"Yes, I always do."

"Try it on. I want you as a valet in tonight's show." I was surprised but exhilarated. I was still at the stage in wrestling where I let my desire to step out from behind that Black Curtain override my good sense.

"There's a bathroom back there," he said, gesturing to the rear of his office.

So I tripped off and threw on my outfit and hurried out.

"I'll need someone to help me lace it up in the back. Do you have a quarter? I'd like to call my husband."

"Oh, you don't need to call him, I can help you with that, honey," he said, smiling as he tossed that night's card aside.

"Um, I don't really feel comfortable having you do that," I said. I did my best to try and sound diplomatic.

"Look, Amanda, I can make you a star, but you have to work with me and meet me halfway. There are certain dues that all the girls have to pay when they get into this business. That is just the way it works. I know you want to get into wrestling really badly and I want to help you. If you let me, I'll introduce you to the right people and make you a star."

I wanted to get into wrestling badly all right, but I knew that Peter was feeding me a line of shit. Even if it were true, and I was pretty sure it wasn't, then I didn't want into professional wrestling *that* badly. I wanted to beat Peter to a pulp for lying to me all of this time, but most of all I just wanted to get out of that auditorium and away from anything that smacked of professional wrestling. As I grabbed my things and left, Peter tried to talk me out of leaving by telling me how much potential I had and so forth and so on. I barely heard half of what he said as I threw the doors open, ran down the steps and across the street, and jumped into my car. All the hard work wasn't for nothing, but it seemed like every time I made a little progress in wrestling, something would happen to powerbomb me back to square one.

I drove for hours all over town. I didn't want to go home and face Donald, who had quite rightly figured out these people long ago. He is sweet and not the sort to say, "I told you so," and in general I have found that when I listen to him things usually go a lot easier for me. Not always, because he can be overly pessimistic where I'm overly optimistic. But between us we strike a nice balance, I think.

Finally, hours later, I parked behind the auditorium and watched the wrestlers as they came out from the show. I don't know why I went back. I sat in my car wallowing in self-pity and despair. I felt like some hopeless protagonist in a Stephen Crane novel. I saw Honky Tonk come out, sign a couple of autographs, and walk to his car. He was wearing an old gray sweatshirt with cut-off sleeves and carrying a black guitar case. A few fans waited for them, hoping for an autograph, or a word of recognition from their heroes of the evening.

"Goodbye, Honky Tonk!" one woman shouted.

"We love you!" a couple of other people yelled.

He happened to walk past my car on the way to his ride.

The look on his face was heartbreaking. I saw a look of intense loneliness on the man's face. His eyes had the vacant look of a man who lives in a world surrounded by people who love the ageing evil Elvis impersonator that he plays, but no one knows or cares about the man behind the act. It all reminds me of a story I heard about Albert Einstein and Charlie Chaplin, when chance happened to put them on a train together in London.

"Einstein! Einstein!" the people outside the train chanted.

"What does this mean?" Einstein asked. He had never been famous before and it had all come very suddenly.

"Nothing. Absolutely nothing," Chaplin replied.

If I'd had a whit of sense left I would have gone home, back to my job writing software manuals, and forgotten all about wrestling. But I had caught the bug and couldn't vomit it up, not without a fight. As fate would have it, that was the last show the Sacramento Valley Wrestling Alliance ever put on. They disappeared after this event and I haven't seen anything about them since. If there is any justice in the world, Peter is reading this right now in a flophouse on Greenhaven Street in Sacramento, nursing a case of shingles. (Can you tell that I'm a little bitter?)

As it turned out Donald was very understanding about the whole thing, though I think he wanted to twist Peter's head off. (It wouldn't have hurt my feelings at all if he had.) But I rededicated myself to my training and firmly decided that I would go to Killer Kowalski's. So I continued hitting the weights, running the jogging track in Curtis Park, and working on my fledgling Web site. But there was a lot of highway between me and the chance to become a wrestler. If I was going to attend wrestling school in Massachusetts, then my husband and I would have to uproot our lives and move to the other side of the country.

CHAPTER FIVE

I HATE BIG RUSTY TRUCKS

STORMDATE: November 27 to December 4, 1998.

"So you really want to do this wrestling thing?" my husband, Donald, asked. "Now, don't take this the wrong way, but if we move 3,500 miles away there's no turning back. I know you understand but I need to say it anyway."

My husband and I were sitting at our living room table reasonably discussing the unreasonable. Should we or should we not move from Sacramento to New England because I wanted to attend Killer Kowalski's Institute of Professional Wrestling?

"Well, I'm not going to give up once we commit to this thing unless I'm in a wheelchair or something like that."

"I know you have put a lot of work into this already," Donald said. He glanced at the list of pros and cons we had made concerning our decision to move.

"Yes."

He searched my eyes for a long moment as he tapped a pencil on the table. Donald nodded a little and tore up the piece of paper between us. We both stood up and embraced. The pencil fell to the floor.

"Then it's decided," he said. "We move to New England."

Once Donald and I had made all of our preparations and said our tearful farewells, we packed all of our belongings into a big yellow truck with our car in tow behind on a trailer. We also had to make room for the cat because neither of us wanted to put her on a flight unattended. We had both heard horror stories of what happens to animals that are relegated to the cargo area, so we just weren't willing to take a chance with our little buddy. Unfortunately for the three of us, we were about to experience a little horror story of our own. Several, actually.

After about two hours on the road I became a little dubious about how hot the engine was running. After about another hour we couldn't use the air conditioner anymore because whenever it was on, the temperature gauge would climb inexorably toward the red. This wasn't good because we were in the middle of Nevada amongst the sand, the buzzards, tumbleweeds, and the occasional cactus. But we did our best to grin and bear it. After all, what is an adventure without a little adversity, right?

Unfortunately, no one could convince our cat, Melissa, that this trip was an adventure. She started crying and howling the moment we put her in the cat carrier in Sacramento

*Ensigns of past
glories*
D.J. VON WYC

and literally didn't stop the whole time we were driving. Donald and I both kind of assumed that she would get tired and cry herself out eventually, but Melissa seemed to have the patience of Job. Eventually we could take no more and reluctantly banished her to the cargo compartment. So much for the cat not riding with the baggage, but Donald was ready to toss her out, carrier and all, on the side of the highway. I can't blame him because I was pretty close to feeling the same way.

Neither Donald nor I had ever driven across the country so on the first day we made a beginner's mistake. Instead of stopping off around 7 p.m., getting a hotel, having a nice dinner, and relaxing, we drove and drove and drove figuring that we would just get a hotel when we couldn't drive anymore. Well, around 11 p.m. that started to seem like a bad idea. Besides the fact that the only trace of civilization in large stretches of Nevada is the I-80 itself, what hotels we did come across were already full. So we were forced to drive and drive some more until Donald, me, and Melissa were all crying out of frustration and fatigue. Then we arrived in lovely Elko, Nevada.

The first thing we noticed about this dusty, rather seedy town was that some guy who was walking down the street started following us as we slowly drove down the main drag looking for a motel that didn't charge by the hour. Then we turned around and our shadow did an abrupt about-face and continued following us. Donald and I just looked at each other and nodded. I bit my lip and steered Old Rusty back onto I-80 again with thoughts of wanting to beat that stranger to death with a baseball bat. Fortunately we were able to find a room just down the road.

We got a late start the next day because we both slept the slumber of the dead and because we couldn't find Melissa. I looked under the bed, which was her usual hiding place when she was scared. No dice. Under the entertainment center, behind the dresser, in the tub, *everywhere*, and no cat. We hadn't opened the door or window so she couldn't have gotten out, but try as we might we couldn't turn up the cat. I was starting to become frightened and upset because despite the fact that I wanted to throttle her, I love my kitty dearly. (I guess I learned a little of what mothers must go through?) Happily Donald came to the rescue when he looked under the bed and noticed her tail poking out from inside the box spring. Apparently the little monster was so desperate not to travel that she had torn a hole in the box spring and climbed up inside. Unfortunately the pills the vet had given us to "take the edge off" her weren't really working.

Day Two on the road started off with a bang. After a few hours driving we got through Salt Lake City. We stopped and I started pumping gas while Donald went inside the store. As I was pumping I noticed that the trailer was on fire! Fire is bad under normal circumstances, but given that I was holding a gas nozzle in my hand this was especially disastrous. I grabbed the fire extinguisher and put out the blaze which apparently started with the now fried brakes and spread to the tire. It was fortunate that we stopped when we did because it looked like the fire had been going for a while. We called the Big Rusty Truck people and they brought out another trailer. What with the wait and moving the car and everything else, we lost almost three hours.

Donald and I were relentless once we got back on the trail and made it through Wyoming. We didn't see much civilization in Wyoming either, though there were a lot of large metal grills that served as wind breaks along the edge of the highway. We also dodged more than one tumbleweed. There were some gorgeous views of mesas and colorful "painted" rock formations that gleamed orange, yellow, and red in the fire of the setting sun. The most remarkable thing about

Wyoming, though, was the incredible gusts that almost forced us off the road on more than one occasion. This was no small thing given that we were in a fully loaded truck hauling a car behind us. But we survived and made it to North Platte, Nebraska, that evening.

Day Three started with Donald peeling Melissa out of the box spring. By early afternoon we were near Lincoln, Nebraska, when tragedy struck. The heating system finally blew and we were stranded on the highway. Donald was able to baby the truck off the highway where we finally came to rest at the bottom of the exit ramp. This was before we had our now ubiquitous cell phones, but Fortune smiled as well as frowned upon us. A very nice woman, who lived in a house across the street from the exit, saw our plight and offered us the use of her phone as well as giving us cold drinks. She was truly an angel.

The police showed up and in assessing the situation asked what we had in the back of the truck.

"Well, we have an animal," I said.

The larger of the two officers bristled a bit.

"What kind of animal, ma'am?"

"My cat."

He instantly relaxed and cracked a big smile. His older, more laid-back partner turned and coughed, trying to hide the fact that he was laughing. I guess he thought Melissa was a tiger or something. (I didn't mention the fact that we actually had enough firepower in the back of our truck to start a small republic in south central Africa.)

Donald drove the truck and I rode with the police as they led us to the nearest Big Rusty Truck service center which was a couple of miles away. They were kind enough to call ahead so that the BRT people would know we were coming. Who says there is never a cop around when you need one?

We basically spent the rest of the day at the service center, where the mechanics tried to fix our truck. Eventually they gave up and declared it a "piece of shit" and informed us that whoever rented us the vehicle was trying to unload a junker. Great. So they got us a new truck and we were forced to unload all of our possessions (again) into the new vehicle, which I must say was much nicer and newer. Both Donald and I were completely demoralized and only got as far as Omaha, which makes me think of *Wild Kingdom* every time.

By Day Four Donald and I were getting used to the rigors of travelling. We were on the outskirts of Iowa City by mid-afternoon when the sky suddenly turned black. The clouds sort of reminded me of a giant, airborne cloud like a squid ejects when it is swimming away from a predator. And what did we see probing down to the earth but a tornado funnel. Fortunately for us the storm seemed to be heading in the other direction because we were soon clear of it and back on our journey.

Day Five literally flew by. Our new truck was proving reliable and we were able to make much better time and by the sixth day your intrepid trio was somewhere in Pennsylvania. I hesitate to say where exactly because of an unlikely incident that makes all of the others seem pedestrian. We were driving along when it became obvious that someone in a beat-up pickup was following us. He was very clearly pacing us, so as to stay behind the truck. When we slowed down, so did the pickup and he sped up when we did. Finally Donald decided to apply the litmus test by pulling off at a rather obscure exit at the last moment. Sure enough the guy in the red pickup almost rolled his vehicle so he could continue following us and in fact drove across the grass strip separating the exit from the highway. He then gunned his way ahead of us and pulled in front of our truck and forced us to stop. This was going to get interesting.

The hair was bristling on the back of Donald's neck. Quite frankly I feel sorry for anyone who gets into a physical confrontation with my husband. The guy jumped out of his car with a big ass knife in his hand and started toward our car. My guess was that he wanted to hold us up, since it was pretty obvious that we had a lot of stuff with us and this was a very lonely stretch of highway. I disappeared into the back of the truck as Donald rolled up his window and locked the door.

When I came back into the cab a few moments later the man was rapping on the window with his knife and making threatening gestures to Donald, who was staring back at him. I quickly unlocked my door, jumped out, and ran around to the side of the truck toward our would-be assailant.

"Throw your knife on the ground," I said in a rather reasonable voice as I pointed my assault rifle at him.

"Oh shit, I was just kidding, honey," he said slowly putting up his hands.

"Uh huh." I spun the rifle around and smashed him in the face with the butt, which forced him to drop the knife. Donald jumped out of cab, kicked the knife in the bushes and literally picked up the guy with one hand. Meanwhile, I pulled out a knife of my own and slashed all of his tires, cut his radiator hose, and ripped out his distributor wires. I took his car keys out of the ignition and put them in my pocket. I still have them to this day as a souvenir.

This next part slays me because I didn't know he had it in him. Donald walked over to the guy's truck and in one quick motion rolled the thing over on its side. I couldn't believe it. I just stood there with my mouth open for a moment and then I started laughing hysterically.

"Come on, hon, let's get out of here," Donald said, putting his arm around me. He looked at the guy for a moment and spit out a harsh, mean laugh that I've only heard come out of him twice now in the five plus years that I have known him. "I guess it wasn't this asshole's lucky day."

The rest of the trip was a cakewalk after that little adventure. We stayed in a Portland hotel for almost a week until we found a nice house for rent in Gray, Maine. It was at the end of a road, screened by lots of trees and with 10 acres for a backyard. Almost the polar antithesis of the box we called home back in Sacramento.

I didn't have much time to rest, though. I was going to be

valeting in a week and starting my training at Killer Kowalski's soon after. So Donald and I spent a week at the lovely Comfort Inn out near the airport in Portland, Maine, while we got ready to move in. Melissa made herself very much at home up inside the box spring.

CHAPTER SIX

"YOU'RE NOTHING BUT A SMALL-TITTED WHORE"

STORMDATE: December 13, 1998.

My hubby and I had been living in Maine for less than a week when it was time to make my first appearance in a wrestling ring. We spent 10 hours in our Honda driving down to Pottsville, Pennsylvania. I had a lot of time to kill, so I tried imagining what my first show would be like, especially behind the scenes.

I was about a week away from starting my wrestling training at Killer Kowalski's, so the promoter worked me in as "protection" for their main, mastermind heel manager, Brian Austin Steele. Apparently, Brian had been having some problems with wrestlers attacking him for no apparent reason. (Unless you count the fact that he and his henchmen were interfering in their matches.) Coincidentally, Brian was also the promoter and a really nice guy behind the scenes. He is someone who loves wrestling and was fun to work for.

But enough kissing up to Brian, at least until he hires me again. (Yes, Brian, that is a hint.) For my first match, I was back-up for "The Highlander" Angus McPhairro. The Highlander was very much your traditional Scotsman: kilt, bagpipe entrance music, black kneepads, that goofy purse Scots wear over their crotch . . . basically the whole haggis. And he was tough, too. Let's face it, you would *have* to be tough getting through life wearing a dress. Especially if, like Angus, you are from New Jersey.

When I walked into the restaurant the first thing I noticed were the 10 guys working on setting up a wrestling ring in the middle of the dining room. There were these two enormous men directing the operation who just *had* to be wrestlers. (They reminded me of Earthquake and Typhoon on the budget plan.) Actually, as it turned out, *all* of the guys putting up the ring were wrestlers. That was my first surprise. It never occurred to me that the workers performing in the ring would be setting the thing up too. Even in Pottsville, Pennsylvania.

I've learned a lot about wrestling rings since Pottsville. Some have springs, others are constructed on the principle of a flexible network of beams. Then you have boxing rings, which feel about as good as hitting a solid wood floor. Heck, these days I own a wrestling ring, but I'm getting a little ahead of myself. When I walked into the Pines restaurant I hadn't so much as set foot in a ring before. I remember thinking, "Ah ha, so they have a *spring* under the ring! So that's why the ring has so much bounce!" as I tried to hide my curiosity behind an air of experienced appraisal. (Remember, this show was before the television stations all began jumping on the professional wrestling exposé bandwagon.)

I was trying to play like this wasn't my first show, so I didn't ask any questions. I just watched while they laid the plywood boards over the framework, then the foam cushioning and finally the canvas. Then they hooked up the ropes. Have you noticed that in boxing rings there are usually four ropes, while wrestling rings have only three? This is because in the rassling game you want to make it easy for the wrestlers to jump, fall, or get pushed out of the ring to the unforgiving floor below. Despite the fact that boxing is starting to become a lot more like professional wrestling with things like ear-biting incidents, they still do try to keep the fighters in the ring.

Once the ropes were tightened the wrestlers piled into the ring to "try it out." One of them, "Earthquake," I think it was, bounced off the ropes, ran across the ring and bounced off the opposite side, finally coming to a stop in the center of the ring. He paused in reflection for a moment, then nodded to himself and climbed out of the ring.

Then came the little guys, who like to jump off the top and do all of those crazy flips where you wonder how they don't get hurt. One of them hopped onto the top rope in the corner and did a moonsault into the middle of the ring. I cringed as he landed on his shoulder. He got up slowly, trying to make-believe that he was something out of an Arnold movie. ("I don't have time to bleed.") There really is no secret to how they keep from getting hurt, because the simple fact is, they *do* get hurt.

"Tighten the top one a little more, OK?" the little guy asked. Those high flyers pretty much like that top rope as tight as you can get it. For my part it doesn't really matter. I simply try to work with whatever fate throws my way. If the ropes are too tight then it is more painful for someone of my size to run them with any authority, so I work more holds and do things like slams. If they are loose, then I stay away from the top altogether.

One thing about wrestling rings is there really is no standard set-up at the independent level. Most are 18´ x 18´ or 20´ x 20´. I have worked a couple as small as 14´ x 14´ and in one monster that was 22´ x 22´. Let me tell you, I felt like I was in a cross-country meet instead of a wrestling match in that big ring. Sometimes the top rope is lower than my shoulder blades and other times it is almost eye level. Now I'm a little over 5´ 7″ so I'm reasonably tall as women go. But the ropes on some rings are so high that I feel like a midget. Anyway, the lesson here with rings is that sometimes the best strategy is to bend like a reed in the wind. Try to fit your style to the circumstances of each night, not the other way around. At that time I didn't really have a "style" but I was curious about everything that was going on. Remember, Plato attributed to Socrates the notion that the wise man is the one who *doesn't* think he already knows everything.

Once the ropes were tightened again, the rest of the wrestlers all jumped into the ring as if they were a pack of jackals pouncing on a rotting carcass. It looked like a battle royale in there with maybe 15 guys punching each other, taking back bumps, putting each other into headlocks, and desperately trying to get in as much ring time as possible before the promoter started letting people through the door.

This is how many wrestlers learn, practice new moves, and in general improve their craft. Unfortunately, a lot of guys can't afford wrestling school. I'm very lucky that my husband was willing to work and allow me to devote an entire year basically to learning everything I could about becoming a wrestler as well as trying to get the word out about Amanda Storm. That kind of support is rare in any circumstance.

It seemed an opportune time to retreat to the dressing room. Now I have gotten ready for shows in some pretty strange places, as you will learn later. But my first dressing room was actually quite nice as such arrangements go, though I was still too clueless to appreciate this fact. We were given a very spacious basement that looked like it was once used for private parties, but was now being used mainly to store food, alcohol, and soda.

The first thing I noticed was the haze of cigarette smoke that hung over the room like a dark, swirling curtain. I never imagined that professional wrestlers were all a bunch of finely tuned athletes, but I was sort of under the impression that they lived reasonably well for the most part. I couldn't have been more wrong. Many a cigarette and even a couple of cigars lost their lives in that dressing room, as did a plethora

Amanda is the brain and the brawn in this trio
D.J. VON WYC

of chips, donuts, and other snack foods. And I don't even want to think about how much money the Coca-Cola company raked in that night from the performers alone. Now I know what Steve Austin meant when he said that wrestlers on the road "eat like billy goats." Personally, I feel that he should apologize to goats everywhere.

Back to the dressing room issue. Naturally the burning question for most of you is if there is only one room where did you and the other women change? Well, happily there was one working bathroom downstairs and we took turns. It was quite a production squeezing into my leather bondage corset, and then I had to have my husband tie it up in the back. I would have hated to go through all of the necessary contortions in front of a bunch of people I didn't know and at my first show to boot. I was scared enough as it was, even though I was doing a pretty good job playing the role of confident valet.

The guys didn't seem to be bothered by the fact that we girls were in their dressing area. Several of the men just matter-of-factly stripped down and changed into their costumes. Like so much else, I didn't realize it at the time but the reality of most professional wrestling shows is that everyone often shares the same dressing room. There isn't always a working bathroom just around the corner. Heck, sometimes there is no bathroom at all.

Personally, I have come to prefer working shows where there is just one dressing room. The problem with having a separate locker room is that there are usually no more than one or two female wrestlers on most independent shows, and it gets pretty boring waiting around with only one other person for company. Especially if you aren't close friends.

"Oh sure," you say. "That's just a bunch of doo-doo. Amanda just likes to see King Kong Bundy naked." While that is undoubtedly true, ogling naked wrestlers is way down there on my list of reasons. If you have read books written by certain other wrestlers, then you know that the workers talk about sex a lot. But one thing I have noticed is that when the pants come off, all of the sex talk pretty much stops. Wrestlers are a pretty flexible bunch of people for the most part, and basic dressing room etiquette dictates that you give people their privacy or at least treat them with a modicum of dignity when they are naked.

The main reason why your modest narrator goes for the co-ed scene is because one gets booked on shows by making contacts with other wrestlers. And most of this connecting for us undercard guys and gals happens in locker rooms during the shows. I can't even begin to count the number of times I have gotten noticed by a new promotion because I have had some permutation of the following conversation with another wrestler:

"Hey, Amanda, you wrestle girls *and* guys too?" Dick the Destroyer asked.

"Yup, I work with anyone. Guys, girls, midgets. Hell, I'll wrestle the ring crew if it gets me on the show."

"Cool." Dick paused a moment and chuckled. "I know this fed down in New York that is looking for workers. I'll give them your number if that's OK by you."

"Sure! Thanks, Richard. There are a couple of feds up my way that are always looking for workers," I said as we exchanged business cards.

I know that pro wrestlers quietly exchanging their business cards out in the back might seem a little strange, but this is how business gets done. So if I am stuck cooling my heels in the women's locker room with only my opponent for company, then both of us are kind of out of the loop. Sure, there might be a few valets knocking around, but most of them are only on the show because they showed up with their boyfriend or husband. No disrespect intended, but for the most part this is the truth.

As I write this, dressing rooms in pro wrestling sort of

remind me of those dystopian, futuristic movies like *Robocop* where they try to emphasize how different things are from the present day by having the sexes matter of factly sharing the same locker room and even showers without the film receiving an X-rating. But, Dear Reader, the future is now because this is exactly what goes on in hundreds of armories, high schools, and town halls all across America every weekend.

The "black curtain" for this establishment was the kitchen, where you had to wait before making your entrance to ringside.

"What's cooking, Chef?" I asked, trying to sound casual.

"Huh? Dunno. Think it's chicken soup." Chef paused from stirring her soup and began rooting through the trash. "Yup, it's chicken!" she said, triumphantly holding up a huge, empty can.

"Coolies!" I grinned as I played with the strands of my flogger. Chef didn't know it but our little conversation helped me a lot. I had managed to take the edge off my pre-match stage fright by talking to her like this wasn't my first time in a wrestling show. I smile when I look back on Pottsville now, but at the time I was absolutely petrified.

The crowd of about 50 people gave Angus, Brian, and myself a nice round of boo's, catcalls, and other abuse as we sauntered around the corner and walked past the bar to the ring. Then it was time for Angus's opponent, who went by the name of Bali Djaka. He was your typical 300-plus pound vampire with long, greasy hair and a moldy, black sweatsuit that made disturbingly loud crackling noises whenever Bali walked. (To tell you the truth, every time I munch on a cracker I think of this guy.) He wasn't exactly my idea of a classic babyface, but this was my first show, so what did I know?

The ring was set up in the middle of the restaurant dining room, and the crowd was seated in chairs not more than four feet from what was about to become "the action." I was standing next to the ring apron, so the people in the front row could have literally reached out and touched me. Fortunately they didn't, but they sure had a lot to say. The people were noisy in a drunk sort of way, but I hadn't really noticed what they were saying when we made our grand entrance. I was too busy hiding my terror behind a mask of leather, muscles, and red hair. I had some time on my hands now though while the classic vampire babyface made his entrance to strains of Megadeth.

"You're a stupid bitch!" one clean cut blonde boy screamed.

"You're a slut!" a chubby little dark-haired girl yelled. Her mother laughed and shouted something I most definitely won't repeat here. Have another beer, honey.

Damn. All the three of us had done was walk out and stand around. And why half the crowd was kids when all of the adults were sitting around drinking beer and harder stuff was beyond me. I guess they know how to party in Pottsville, Pennsylvania!

"Shut your filthy mouth, you scums!" I yelled at the howling mob.

"Fuck you, you're nothing but a small-titted whore!" a boy yelled. God, this kid could have been a poster boy for

Wassup?
MIKE HOLMES

the Mormons or something. He couldn't have been more than eight, but what a potty mouth! Really now. They weren't that small.

I saw a large, dark shape lumbering up behind me. It was Djaka and he was about three feet away from me. Bali couldn't just walk past me like I wasn't there, but as a babyface it would have been very bad if he had pushed or hit me at this point. After all, I hadn't actually done anything to him yet and good guys — even the undead — aren't generally supposed to hit women.

"YOU'RE NOTHING BUT A SMALL-TITTED WHORE"

So I spun around like I hadn't seen him and beat feet to the other side of the ring. It was just as well because I wanted to get far away from "small-titted whore" boy. I pumped my arms sort of like I was race-walking as I scuttled away from Bali and hid behind a Christmas tree not too far from the ring. I didn't think of it at the time because I was operating on pure instinct, but afterwards I got a chance to see the match on tape and to be honest I was very pleased with my reaction. (Actually, I was happy that I didn't get flustered and just stand there.)

The match started off conventionally enough with Brian directing a few comments at Djaka, which caused the "vampire" to turn his back on Angus. One might say that Brian distracted him, but I have found that such things almost always depend upon one's point of view. McPhairro jumped all over his opponent quickly with kicks, punches, and forearms.

I stood near the ring while the two wrestlers went back and forth in a fairly even contest. I had never been part of a match before, but I had watched a lot of wrestling shows and taken notes to help prepare myself for my first gig as a manager. One important thing that I noticed is that the good managers don't yell, scream, and in general get all crazy when the wrestlers are flying all over the building. But let Angus get Bali in some sort of hold down on the mat, and the managers go nuts howling at the crowd to get them worked up and keep them interested in the match. I didn't understand the theory behind the principle at the time, but that is the strategy I followed and it worked.

Mostly I followed Brian around a lot and acted like I was

his personal bodyguard. Naturally he would get in a few cheap shots on Djaka whenever the referee's back was turned or Angus was able to distract him. At the time I remember thinking that "Brian Austin Steele" was a great manager. He was small and kind of goofy-looking in an anemic, Larry Bird-on-the-budget-plan sort of way, but best of all everything he did looked furtive and cheap. Especially his punches. And 15 months of wrestling school and over 200 of my own matches later, I stand by my assessment. Brian is a great manager and was probably the one most responsible for getting the people behind the rather unsympathetic Bali Djaka.

Bali was finally able to overcome McPhairro's admittedly creative interpretations of the rules, as well as Steele's interference and the moral support I was lending the cause by standing around in my leather corset and yelling a lot. He bounced Angus all over the ring with punches, kicks, clotheslines, and slams, and the vampire even threw in a low dropkick to the prone Scotsman's back. Brian, seeing his man in trouble, jumped up on the ring apron and started arguing with the referee while the vampire was pinning his opponent. Djaka waited for the referee's count, which of course never came. I started mocking Bali and jerking the people's chain by counting outside the ring. I got up to seven before the referee regained his senses. (Have you ever noticed how fragile the officials are in professional wrestling?)

Bali definitely wasn't the brightest penny in the piggy bank but eventually he figured out how things stood. He got up, shoved the ref out of the way, and decked poor Steele, who ran up the scales to about 140 pounds soaking wet. This was where your humble narrator came in. I tossed my whip to McPhairro, who was still stunned in the middle of the ring. Of course the only people who noticed were the 50 fans in attendance at ringside. (Officials are also notoriously blind as well as wimpy.)

"He's got her whip!" the kids screamed. Excellent. The fans were reacting exactly as we wanted. "Watch out!" Naturally vampire boy was so absorbed in his discussion with the zebra that he was completely oblivious to the fans. Angus milked the moment for all it was worth as he skulked up behind Djaka and slowly raised my flogger.

"He's right behind you!"

"Shut up! Shut up! Shut up!" I howled. I embellished the moment by hopping around, waving my arms, and gesticulating wildly. They were getting louder and louder, but when Angus McPhairro laid into the back of vampire boy's skull with the butt of my whip the place erupted. I never realized that 50 people could make so much noise, even if you factor in that most of them were drunk. He tossed the weapon back out of the ring to yours truly, and I hid it behind my back and scuttled off to my hiding place behind the Christmas tree. The referee recovered just in time to beat out the count and raise the Scotsman's hand in victory. Angus bailed out of the ring and we made our way out in triumph past the screaming kids and their drunken parents. We were truly the evil wrestling gods of Pottsville, Pennsylvania, if only for the briefest of moments.

Phew, we survived and made our way back through the kitchen and down the stairs to our dressing room.

"Did ya win?" Chef asked as we sauntered on past.

"Oh yes, we're superstars now," I winked at her and patted Brian on the back.

I perched on a stack of cases of Jack Daniels and tried to become one with the paneling. I didn't really know how I should act in a dressing room yet, so I figured that the best thing to do was sit quietly and wait. I did my best to maintain my outer facade of calm as I watched Bali and Angus doing a little post-coital hugging and laughing about their match.

"Hey, good job," Angus said as he walked past me.

"Thanks," I replied, trying to sound nonchalant, but inside I was clicking my heels for joy.

On a completely different note, I wasn't the only valet in Pottsville appearing in her first show. This girl who called herself "Sage" sat down beside me. "Hi," Sage giggled a little as her eyes darted around the room.

"Hi," I listened to a skinny guy, who was also a vampire, talking about making his entrance to the ring in a body bag. Damn, there sure were a lot of guys making believe they were undead on this show. I don't mean this in a negative way but I was starting to wonder if these guys played a little too much Dungeons & Dragons on weekends when they weren't doing shows.

"How are you?" She giggled some more. I was starting to wonder if this girl was going to make a pass at me, until I realized she just needed someone to talk to. "Does it bother you when people call you names?"

"What do you mean?" I leaned up against the wall and breathed a sigh of relief.

"When you're out there and people are yelling at you, does it bug you?"

"No." I didn't really know what to say. I could see that she was upset and scared. She obviously needed reassurance from another woman who had more experience. I didn't have the heart to tell her that this was my first show.

"How come? I really hate it when they call me 'Thunder Thighs.'" Sage crossed her arms and sighed. My heart went out to her because I could see that she was an unhappy person who didn't really want to be a valet. I found out later that she was at the show because of her wrestler boyfriend, and naturally she was his valet.

Sage, I don't know if you'll ever read this or even if you will remember our little conversation. Perhaps you stuck to your decision not to get involved in wrestling, or maybe you persevered and have since learned the score. In any case, a lot of time has passed and I'd like to give you a better answer to your question than "No."

You have to realize that the part you play as a heel or the chaperone of a heel is primarily that of a public whipping girl. Your job basically boils down to making the people hate you and especially the wrestler you are with, so that they will love and root for the babyface. And the babyface's job is to be loveable and make the fans feel sorry for her when the heel is beating her up. Ideally, the heel *wants* the fans to call her names, scream, and in general come unglued with loathing at the mere sight of her.

My instructor at Killer Kowalski's, Mike Hollow, had this to say when I asked him about heels and babies:

"The heel represents the fan's unpaid bills, their boss, and their ex who cheated on them. The babyface is Christmas, New Year's, and Easter all rolled into one. The job of each wrestler is to sell himself and his opponent to the fans. Think of the baby as someone who passes out candy to each of the fans. The heel is the asshole who comes along and tries to take away that candy. A match is a popularity contest and neither wrestler wins unless they both get over." There is a surprising amount of theory behind a good wrestling match and I have learned and continue to learn a lot of my theory from Mike. For Amanda Storm personally, every "Fuck you" is an "I love you," though I have to admit it disturbs me a little when people let their eight year olds flip me the bird in public or call me a "small-titted whore."

Sage, you have to expect that people will pick out your flaws and make fun of you for them. Naturally our most obvious imperfections are the physical ones. So if you have heavy legs as a heel then of course the fans are going to make fun of them. I wouldn't feel bad about it. Heck, sometimes I even accentuate my physical flaws because I want the fans to make fun of me. And when they do, believe me, I yell and scream, bitch at the referee, wave my arms around wildly, and threaten to leave the match. All of this just makes them get on my case more, which is very good for both Amanda Storm and her opponent. If I lose the match then great, because the fans want to see me lose. If I win even better, because now they are pissed off. So when the next match comes they should be all primed up to root for the next babyface, because I have taken away the fan's candy and they want it back.

If you are having a problem with something, Sage, a good way of looking at it is that there is always someone who has it worse. If you are limping, there is someone who can't walk and if you can't walk, there are plenty of people in cemeteries who can do even less. Take poor Walter Kowalski for example. He started out as a babyface but he was just so big and mean-looking that he had a hard time garnering any sympathy from the fans. So he became a heel and things became more interesting for him. Apparently, he was so good at his job he had to sneak out of the back of wrestling shows to avoid irate fans who wanted to beat him up with their fists and even baseball bats. (I could be wrong, but something tells me that Walter didn't have a "Killer" vanity plate on his car.) So the next time someone makes fun of your weight, Sage, just be thankful that they aren't waiting in the parking lot with broken bottles and baseball bats.

CHAPTER SEVEN

"AMANDA, YOU DUMB BROAD!"

STORMDATE: December 1998 (to the present).

For the next few weeks my wrestling life consisted entirely of wrestling school, and of course working on my body. Despite my best efforts, before I started training in Malden, Massachusetts, my only experience in a professional wrestling show was strictly behind the scenes and helping on the ring crew, except for the valet gig in Pottsville.

The three major skills for being a successful professional wrestler are "having a look," being interesting on the microphone and with your character, and of course being able to wrestle. Of the three, the general consensus is that the "look" is probably the most important, while excelling in the ring is the least, as long as you can do a few things well and have good opponents to work with. But it has always been and remains my ambition to excel in all three areas, so I spend a lot of time working on what they call "all aspects of being a wrestler."

People often ask me what wrestling school is like; it is probably the question I am asked by fans the most, especially women. I have had the opportunity to train as a guest in other schools and each time it leaves me with a new appreciation of Kowalski's. I visited a "school" once that was literally a bunch of old, moldy gymnastic mats with clothesline substituting for ropes in some guy's basement. The instruction consisted of being tossed around by the "trainer," who wasn't particularly competent himself. The emphasis was on proving you were tough or "hardcore" enough to be a wrestler rather than on acquiring anything in the way of skills. It looked more like an S&M session than wrestling. Needless to say, I took a pass on participating and remained an "interested spectator." (Well, I did give one of the new guys a few stiff chops but that was it.)

That gym was an extreme but I have visited a lot of schools where even little Amanda was clearly a cut above the trainer in terms of wrestling skill, and that scares me. Don't get me wrong, I am very proud of what I am able to do in the ring for the amount of time I have been in the business. But if I am a better wrestler than a "veteran" who is supposed to be teaching this stuff, then something is desperately wrong. It would be like me walking into a dojo with some karate under my belt and blowing away the guy who supposedly is the "master." Something would most definitely stink in the state of Denmark, don't you think?

Despite the bad ones, there are some good wrestling schools out there and Killer Kowalski's is certainly one of them. The students train in a well maintained professional ring and the instruction is top notch. Not only do they teach you how to wrestle, Mike Hollow and Walter teach you how to protect yourself and your opponent, and in general prepare you to succeed as a wrestler.

I remember the first day I went to Walter's and started training. I climbed those marble stairs to the sound of guys taking bumps in the ring. My heart leapt with each crash and with every stair I climbed. Here was the reason we picked up our lives and moved from California to New England. Could I hack it? What if I wasn't tough enough, strong enough, or whatever enough to make it? How could I explain it to my husband? "Sorry honey for moving all the way out here. Yes, I know we don't know anybody. Uh huh. But I can't really do this wrestling thing and I would like to go back to Sacramento." Nope. Failure just wasn't an option.

So I put those doubts out of my mind as I stood in front of the white doors that separated me from the gym, took a deep breath, and walked inside for the first time with a confident smile on my face. There was Walter sitting in his chair by the entryway watching a few of the veterans running through an impromptu match before class. Mike was over by the ring talking to a couple of the newer students. It was a small class because it was the week before Christmas and the school would be closing down for a couple of weeks. But there were four classes scheduled before the break and

Am I the only normal person here or what?
SUSAN WHITNEY

I wanted to get started as soon as possible.

Once class started Mike had everyone introduce themselves and welcome me to the school. Then I went over to a
corner with a guy named Darren who went through some of
the most basic moves, like how to lock up correctly and so on.
Darren was a very patient teacher and I learned a lot from him
in my first session. Darren's main claim to wrestling fame —
at least so far as I know — is that he wrestled Chyna when she
was in the independents, but not exactly in what you'd call
traditional matches. One of Darren's wrestling names is
"Raindrop"; he puts on a mask and competes in "women's"
matches. Needless to say one of my major ambitions in

wrestling was to win Killer Kowalski's All Star Wrestling women's title and defend it successfully against Raindrop. (My dream was half-fulfilled when I recently refereed a match in which Raindrop unsuccessfully challenged Violet Flame for the women's title.)

All in all the class went great and I was excited and energized about wrestling. I had learned a few moves and at Mike's suggestion I took notes and started a "wrestling notebook" which continues to grow to this day. Who knows, if I am lucky and have a good career maybe it will be worth some money when I retire?

In one of the early classes I learned how to flip over the top rope backwards. It is a move I do a lot now — mainly because I don't see many American women doing it — but at the time learning this relatively simple move was a major challenge. I wouldn't do it quite right and instead of going over the rope I'd just end up flopping around and hurting my lower back. Once you are over the top rope, there is a way you are supposed to push your body away from the ring so you don't come crashing down into the ring apron, which really hurts (trust me on this one, boys) and is very dangerous. It amazes me when I occasionally see experienced guys on WWF shows not "taking care of themselves" when they perform this maneuver.

The first time I succeeded in getting over the top rope, I didn't push away and came crashing down into the side of the apron. It hurt but fortunately I happened to hit myself where I was wearing a lot of padding so I wasn't injured. Trust me, when a wrestler comes crashing down so her hip meets the side of the ring, it isn't the ring that says, "Ouch!" Mike held his breath for a second and asked me if I was OK. I nodded that I was and just kind of stood there for a second, mentally "checking" everything to make sure I wasn't hurt.

Well, Walter jumped out of his chair and ran over to me. I remember thinking at the time that he could move awfully fast when he was motivated considering that he has to be pushing 75. "Amanda, you dumb broad, do it right and you won't get hurt!" he screamed like two inches from my face. "If you want to be a wrestler you have to learn to protect yourself!"

"Yes, Sir," I squeaked. He shook his head and mumbled something as he slowly walked back to his chair, apparently relieved that his new student was still in one piece.

"Do it again!" Mike said in his stern, instructor tone of voice.

That is one thing about Mike Hollow. When you talk to him outside of the school or training, he is a real sweetie. (I can say that about him because I'm a woman.) But when he is teaching, he takes on a very different tone. He becomes almost like a drill sergeant and very authoritarian, but in a way the students respect because we all know he only wants us to improve and meet our potential. I was in the military myself some years ago and I recognize that Mike is employing the exact demeanor that successful officers and NCOs use with their subordinates. And to his credit Mike has made me cry only once, and that was my own fault because I was stupid and came to the school a few days after I had had a death in the family. (I wasn't in the emotional shape for wrestling and I should have just stayed home that week. Poor, Mike, I made him feel like a total heel. But I digress as usual.) So I did the maneuver again and remembered to push away this time. Walter nodded slightly, Mike gave me a word of praise, and the next person stepped up for his turn.

The basic pattern of my training at school is, we start out doing conditioning drills and warming up, then move to performing spots. We might pair up and sometimes Mike makes the match-ups himself to combat the natural tendency people have to train with their friends. One of the important skills a wrestler needs to learn early on is the ability to work with almost anyone, and certainly people you have never stepped in the ring with before. These days I am constantly wrestling people I have never met before, and if my training consisted only of pairing up with the students I was comfortable with, then I would be ill prepared for the challenge indeed.

We continue doing spots, and the newer guys might not participate in some of the more complicated ones right away. Instead they will either just learn one of the moves in the spot, do something easier, or just watch. For example, we might start out with some quick drills to get warmed up. Everyone in class will get in a line and take turns jumping through the ropes, then going through the ropes to the outside of the ring backwards, and finally over the top rope both forwards and backwards.

Then each of us will get a partner and do a quick easy drill. A common one is to lock up, my guy powers me to the ropes and then shoots me off, and I take a clothesline in the middle of the ring. He goes for the quick pin but I kick out on one. He jumps to his feet and runs at me going for my head, but I sweep out his legs and pin him. He kicks out and we circle and lock up again. This time I take him to the ropes and repeat the same sequence but we switch roles.

Next we'll add more moves to the spot. So after the second pin, the person doing the pinning will come at the other wrestler and take a quick arm drag, stagger up for another arm drag, and get to his feet a third time only to get scooped up and slammed for his efforts. By the time the class is ready for a water break, we have all performed what would make for a good, solid opening for a singles match.

During the next phase of the class Mike and Walter often teach us some new moves or maneuvers we know but can't necessarily execute well. Back body drops, gut wrench suplexes, and power slams are all moves that come to mind. While we are doing this, the newest students will re-group on the other side of the gym with one of the veterans and work on some of the most fundamental building blocks for learning the craft of wrestling: body and foot positioning when they lock up or put their partner in a headlock; how to put a wrestler in a top wrist lock, who in turn counters by putting his "opponent" in a hammerlock.

Then Mike might pair us up and we'll put together short matches. Some of us will have singles matches and there will usually be one tag match as well. He will assign who are the heels and faces, usually whatever role one is currently working

Mike Hollow: A fount of wrestling wisdom
D.J.VON WYC

in shows. As the title of the book implies, I have been cast mostly as the "bad girl," but I've been increasingly asked to perform as a babyface since lately most of my opponents have been men.

This brings up a point about training which I feel is very important and Mike brings this up all the time. When I am training, I try to act as if there were a crowd watching my every move. When I jump out of the ring, I might try to look angry or afraid. When I vault into the ring I will thrust my arms into the air and yell, "I love you!" and then point out at the audience which generally consists of Walter and maybe two guys who are thinking about joining the class. Or I'll jump up after giving a guy a big slam and show boat, flex my arms, and in general carry on like a lunatic.

Sure, some of the guys get a kick out of my antics and a few of the boys who don't understand what I'm doing probably think I'm showing off. I must admit that sometimes I feel a little goofy professing my wrestling love for a group of imaginary people. But the real reason I "act out" in class is because of the very simple principle that just as "you are what you eat," you also wrestle the way you practice. So I work on expressing myself and being athletic all at the same time.

This has really paid off for me on shows. I do try to move around in the ring and give the people their money's worth in terms of putting together solid matches, but what the fans seem to really respond to in my performances is how I act. They tell me that they like the fact that I really know how to wrestle, but they especially love my character.

And that is the proverbial bottom line in wrestling — that the fans enjoy what you do. I don't care how many high-flying moves a wrestler performs in a match or how vicious his powerbomb looks. If the fans are not interested in the combatants they aren't going to get into the match. Projecting an interesting personality hooks the people into watching your match and solid wrestling is what keeps them entertained. So wrestlers who work on both of these aspects are far more likely to have successful matches and build fan interest than wrestlers who only concentrate on their character or just going through the moves.

I went to class every Tuesday and Thursday night pretty

faithfully for the better part of my first year. This wasn't easy, because I lived in Maine and the drive was over two hours each way. My husband and I both noticed that the closer one got to Massachusetts, the more it was like Sacramento with all of its urban problems, and neither one of us wanted to live in that environment again. So despite the effort, the drive was worth it to me. In a way, it was a good preparation for wrestling because today I routinely drive seven hours or longer each way to get up in front of a crowd and wrestle for 10 minutes. This is part of the price I pay to perform every week and it is worth every moment on the road. But getting used to that Maine to Boston commute during my first days of wrestling school really helped.

These days my wrestling schedule is very busy so I can only make weekday class occasionally, but I do try to go to class one day on the weekends when I'm passing through Boston on my way to or from a wrestling show. The weekend class is a little different. When Mike isn't there, Walter teaches the class with a little help from some of the veteran students. Walter tends to teach a lot of martial arts moves that he has adapted slightly for professional wrestling. I remember a couple of months ago learning a couple of throws from Walter in class. Later on I just happened to be leafing through a book on traditional Chinese wrestling at a bookstore and what did I find but the same moves that Walter had taught me in class!

Walter also knows that I do submission wrestling as well as professional style, so he is always showing me nerve holds, how to tweak pressure points, and that sort of thing. Not too long ago Walter (and this man is in his 70s) had me put him in a body scissors. Well, not only did he get out of it, but he had me literally jumping up to get away from him. This is great stuff to know and I feel lucky to have such good teachers.

Sometimes we would also practice our mike skills by lining up and cutting heel and face interviews. My interviews tend to defy categorization as either face or heel, really. My philosophy for expressing myself on a microphone or in front of a camera has always been to get a concept in my mind and go with it. I don't memorize lines unless the promoter has something specific he or she wants me to say. (In Canada this is usually variations on the "I love Canada" or the "QUAbec sucks!" theme.) For example, say I'm asked to play a crazy person. Well, the last time I did that in class I started off as a traditional face. I talked about my opponent who was supposedly "schooled in the arts of black magic" and was reputed to cast hexes on people. Naturally I didn't believe in such things and was looking forward to showing her a little Amanda Storm magic of my own in the ring.

Suddenly my hand was possessed by the spirit of a lady wrestler from the past whose name I won't repeat here out of respect. My own hand then took on a life of its own, much like the title character in *Dr. Strangelove*, and attacked me. I concluded the interview by rolling around on the floor gurgling out my desire for revenge with my own left hand firmly attached to my throat.

I took a lot of bumps in my early training, which is the usual pattern, and sometimes I still do, but my pattern of training has changed quite a bit since I started going to Kowalski's in December, 1998. I have been working on average two or three live shows a week now for quite some time. With the live shows and the hundreds of miles on the road each week, I find that I can't take the bumps in training like when I first started. Ken Shamrock was right when he said that professional wrestling will slowly grind you down if you don't pace yourself, and that was what I found was happening to me. I try to avoid taking bumps doing maneuvers that I can do in my sleep, because I get all of the practice I need doing these moves at live shows. Instead I work on spots that I want to do in shows and moves that I'm shaky on.

I have also decided to vastly increase the number of moves I know and can perform well, even if I never use them in live shows. I think that teaching is in my future some years down the road and I want to be ready when that time comes. Besides, I want to learn and pass on all of those crazy moves that Walter knows and still invents on a regular basis. Now every class I ask Walter or someone to show me a new move that I work into my practice as best I can and write down in my notebook so I don't forget the steps. So far this strategy has worked very well for me.

Speaking of guys, it is time I addressed another common question people ask me all the time: What is it like as a woman training at a wrestling school? Well, when I first started there were a couple of other women. I remember this one short girl with loads of tattoos, black hair, and a bit of a chip on her shoulder. For some reason she kept comparing me to Chyna

*I owe some homemade bread
and kisses for the man
behind the smile*
ALEXANDRA WHITNEY

and then saying, "You ain't Chyna!" as if I had brought up the subject. She was one of the girls who came and went in my first few months at Kowalski's. A lot of the guys melt away too after a few weeks, but I notice the women more because I'm usually the only one in class.

Then there was another gal who was a veteran and has been in the business for, oh, six years or so. I have learned from her many of the holds and counters I now use, and she is always game when I want to monkey around with something new. She is a really great person and has one of the best attitudes of anyone I have ever met in wrestling so far, and until she moved to the other side of the country, I continued to wrestle her occasionally in matches for various promotions in Massachusetts. Unfortunately she didn't really come to wrestling school anymore and she apparently has some physical problems from an old injury that holds her back now.

So for the last six months or so I have consistently been the only woman training in an otherwise all-male class. Also, with the exception of a few things I have picked up from other women on shows from time to time, all of my training has come from men. I'm not sure if this is a good or bad thing but it is the fact of the matter for me and probably for a lot of women wrestlers.

When I first started at Kowalski's the male students pretty much looked at me as another chick who would probably be gone in a few months or who would just sit on the sidelines. Most of them were cordial, though a little distant at first. I worked hard to change that by trying my best to do everything the rest of the class did. I did the same number of push-ups and squats and participated in all the drills, took the same bumps, and made a lot of the same mistakes as everyone else. And got yelled at like everyone else. Mike was very careful to not give me any special treatment, but at the same time insisted that I be given the same respect as everyone else. For that I can only say, "Thank you."

After a while most of the guys loosened up and were friendly. Some of them would offer me constructive criticism and once they got used to having me around they involved me in their matches before or after class.

Sure, I would occasionally have a problem. A few months ago there was this one newer student who said, "I could never wrestle a woman. I'm afraid I would hurt her."

"That is the chance we all take," I replied. "If she is a worker then she knows the risks, and she'd feel bad if she hurt you too." I happened to be standing right next to him at the time so I couldn't just ignore the comment.

We were both polite, but I could tell that he was uncomfortable with my presence at the school. But I have found that you catch more flies with honey than by screaming at them, so I let him know how I felt in no uncertain terms. We didn't get too heated, and agreed to disagree. But over the last few months he has apparently gotten used to me and we don't have any problems. So ladies, don't take it too personally if some of the boys take a couple of months to bend their minds around having women participating with them in what essentially is a close contact sport. I try to remember that having a woman taking part in what otherwise is a masculine space (to use a term from one of my women's studies classes) is as new for the guys as it is for me.

The one thing that I have pretty much done for myself in wrestling is get myself booked on shows. When Walter puts on a show under his Killer Kowalski's All Star Wrestling promotion, he has always been kind enough to include me as part of his card, both in women's and mixed matches. When I first started wrestling, I worked almost exclusively for a small promotion in Maine that ran shows about once a month. A few months later I branched out to some of the small Massachusetts-based promotions, mainly because some of my female counterparts needed opponents and their regular partners weren't available. Like most other independent wrestlers

I have acted as my own agent and promoter. So word of mouth and having a good reputation with other wrestlers is the key to getting work on shows. But word of mouth won't take you very far if no one knows who you are, and that for me is where the Internet has come in.

I have used the Internet to contact promoters directly and I have had a lot of success getting booked onto shows by using this approach. Lately, however, I have been very fortunate because promoters have come looking for me instead of the other way around. They like what they see on my Web site and might have heard my name on the MTV special (more on that later) or from being in magazines and newspapers, and we move right to negotiating my price, travel arrangements, and so on. I have gotten a lot of work lately in New York, New Jersey, Pennsylvania, and Canada using this approach. As things stand, soon after I am finished writing this book I might be making my debut as a wrestler in California because a wrestling promotion and I sort of found each other over the Internet. Naturally I'm very excited by the prospect. If things work out it will be the first time my family will have an opportunity to see me perform live. In a way it will be like coming full circle.

CHAPTER EIGHT

"JESUS, TONY, SHE AIN'T GOT NO TITS!"

STORMDATE: January, 1999.

Counting the Christmas break, I had been training at Killer Kowalski's for a little under a month. I wasn't a wrestler yet, but I had managed to get myself booked on my first show as a wrestler for an outfit called the Eastern Wrestling Alliance. I had been completely candid with the promoter and told him that this would be my first match, so he planned accordingly. They basically tailored a series of short appearances to introduce me to the fans as a wrestler new to their organization, while doing their best to hide the fact that I was inexperienced in the extreme. The best thing was that the match was in the Lewiston, Maine, armory, which was about 40 minutes from my house.

I was "scheduled" to wrestle Jamie West for the women's title but Jamie didn't show up for our match. I found out later that Jamie wasn't actually booked on the show, though the promoter made it sound like she *had* been booked and just didn't bother coming. Personally I think what the promoter did was wrong. A wrestler's reputation is very important and to tell 500 people that someone didn't show up for a match when they weren't even *called*, just to shoot an angle, isn't right. I think it would have been better to have used another angle that didn't involve besmirching someone's reputation. But what could I say? It was my first match so I just showed up and did what I was told.

I strode out right at the end of a little ceremony where the "vice president" of the federation had given some kid a trophy for being the Fan of the Month. My cue was to come down the ramp just as the boy was walking away with his award. He was adorable, too. I could see that he was thrilled to have his 30 seconds in the spotlight and I was happy for him. Believe me, I knew how he felt.

"Where's my match?" I bellowed into the mike. "I came all the way from Sacramento, California, to wrestle and you can't find an opponent for Amanda Storm? What kind of creep joint is this anyway?" I don't think those were my exact words but you get the general idea.

Mr. Vice President stammered out an apology and I waved my arms around a lot and tried to look pissed off. This was the first time I had gotten any "mike time" and I was terrified. Fortunately my voice didn't break. *That* would have been awful.

"Try to talk more into the microphone," he mumbled as I took the mike away from him and continued my little hissy fit.

*Jack Crow gets
ready to face
the mat*
SUSAN WHITNEY

As promos go I have seen far worse, but it wasn't exactly one for *The Best of Amanda Storm* tape. But you have to start somewhere and this was the beginning of my journey. All in all I thought it went about as well as could be expected.

"I'll be back!" I snarled as I shoved the mike into Mr. Vice President boy's chest and jumped out of the ring. I laugh thinking about it now, because one learns this maneuver on the first day of wrestling school. But at the time I had to concentrate on my little jump through the ropes as if it were something difficult. I was so proud that I hit it. I'm kind of embarrassed to admit this, but after the show I replayed that moment over and over again from a tape that my husband made. Like I said, you have to start somewhere, and most beginnings are pretty humble.

Later in the show the booker decided to have me participate in a run-in of a match between one Kid USA and some other guy. I don't remember his name, though I think he used to wrestle Scott Taylor before he went to the WWF. The angle they were shooting was one where Amanda Storm makes such a nuisance of herself that the "office" is forced to give her a match. They had a weekly half-hour television show, so my appearances were going to be spaced out in the overall televised storyline in order to introduce and (hopefully) get me over with the fans. This was how I explained my motivation afterwards on my Web site:

> I decided to up the "bitch-factor" in hopes that I would get my match. In other words, I hoped the vice president would become so upset with me that he would send out someone, *anyone* out for me to fight, probably with the hope that he/she/it would kick my fat ass all the way back to Sacramento. I had an epiphany of sorts right before the Kid USA match. Now nothing against Kid, but he is one of those buff, boy-toy wrestlers one sees so much of at wrestling shows these days. You know the type, a "fan-favorite" — especially with the teenage girls who are into the fact that he is masculine in a non-threatening way. Need I say more?

So I went out with Robbie Ellis and a manager by the name of Rotten Robbie during the match and proceeded to beat Kid usa down. (Actually, Ellis and the other guy did the beating while I jumped up and down, trying not to trip over the broken particle board "tables" that were laying near the ring.) Then I helped them handcuff Kid, who was outside the ring, to the bottom rope. I had purchased a set of leg irons from a mail order company in New Hampshire a few weeks before and they were really coming in handy. They had a longer chain than regular cuffs, which made them perfect for wrestling. Then I gave the two wrestlers one of my whips and they took turns laying in strokes across Kid's back. The crowd loved it, of course.

Enter Dave Vicious and some other guy. Dave was the resident top babyface, who came out to be the hero of the moment. The two heel wrestlers scampered off to the back while I jumped into the ring and began to taunt Kid usa. I didn't really have any specific instructions, so I started doing a little foot-stomping dance where I made like I was trying to put the leather to his hands. To be honest, Kid wasn't really into this entire angle and just sort of stood there with a sour look on his face. So I started trying to step on his hands for real. He started jumping around pretty good then, saying, "I'm going to kill you, Amanda! You just wait until we get in the back!" I basically ignored his threats and made a mental note to dig the brass knuckles out of my "props bag" in case he was serious. (I broke a guy's jaw with them about ten years ago when I used to ride with a motorcycle club out on the West Coast, who shall remain forever nameless.)

Dave ran off the two heels but he then threw up his hands and stood beside Kid USA, who was still shackled to the ropes. Vicious, being a major babyface, wasn't about to climb up into the ring and beat up a woman, even an obnoxious bitch like me who was basically challenging him or anyone else in the building to "do their worst." Enter Mr. Vice President again, right on cue.

"Cease and desist, Storm!" he yelled, "and give me the key!"

"Give me a match and you can have it!" I screamed back. I dangled the key, which was on a piece of cord, in front of him and then stuffed it down my top and jumped out of the ring. VP boy gave chase of course, though not being a wrestler he couldn't do that quick jump out of the ring like I did. Once we got through the curtain and into the back, he started begging me for the key.

"OK, Storm, I'll give you your match. Just give me the key," he said as he fell to his knees. I paused and enjoyed the moment as he put his arms around my knees and whimpered softly. Nothing turns me on more than a man who is good at groveling. The best part was watching him stride back through the curtain, holding up the key like he was a poor man's Achilles or something. Nothing is funnier than watching a guy as he busily tries to salvage his shattered masculine ego. . . .

That was how I told the story on my Web site. Actually, it went a little differently. I hit the curtain and kept going into the back. My adrenaline was still pumping like crazy, and I was overjoyed that I didn't completely screw up. A couple of the guys, who knew this was my first time on the microphone, patted me on the back and gave me a few words of encouragement as I blew by them.

I got almost all the way back to the dressing room when Mr. Vice President shouted to me. "Amanda!" he said, laughing a little as he caught up and stopped me by putting his hand on my shoulder. "Kid's still out there and we can't unchain him from the ropes."

"Oh shit!" I fumbled around in my bra for the key, which

Aw, you love it and
you know it
D.J. VON WYC

107

I had attached to a long piece of rat tail cord so I wouldn't lose it. A wave of panic started to wash over me. I could not find the key. It apparently had fallen out of my outfit while I was performing.

"Uh, well, this is interesting," I said softly as I continued to feel around for the key. Mr. Vice President didn't say anything, but I could tell that he was becoming a little concerned himself.

I was contemplating whether or not the janitor had access to a good set of bolt cutters when I finally found the key. It had worked its way around to the back of my bra, and the cord was dangling down my back. I handed the precious bit of metal to my fellow performer, who quickly turned and strode back through the curtain to the immediate cheers of the fans. Phew. I would have hated to leave poor Kid USA standing there at ringside, handcuffed to the ropes until the end of the show. I suppose they could have always undone one of the turnbuckles and gotten him out that way, but I suspect that would have impacted negatively on my future employment with this particular federation.

With the key found, I had probably another hour before my "match" so I began my descent into the bowels of the Lewiston Armory to the women's bathroom. As I was about to turn a corner I heard Tony Atlas talking to someone. I could tell by the sound of his voice that it was James St. Jean. Tony was the booker, which among other things meant that he was supposed to decide which wrestlers were on the show. James was the promoter, which basically meant that it was his money and his show. Their conversation wasn't exactly what I would call heated, but I could tell that St. Jean was a little agitated. I stopped and was about to turn around and leave when I heard something that stopped me in my tracks.

"Tony, that Storm doesn't look anything like her pictures," St. Jean said. "The girl said she couldn't wrestle in that leather thing before you ever hired her." (St. Jean was talking about my black bondage corset, of course.)

"What the fuck? This is just what I need. Jesus, Tony, she ain't got no tits!"

One thing I have always found a little annoying about America is the fascination with big boobs. I don't say this because of a long-standing neurosis stemming from not exactly being a prime candidate for a *Busty Beauties* centerfold. I say this because when I got into wrestling I was kind of under the delusion that what I did in the ring was mainly about how I moved, talked, and acted. Now don't get me wrong. I understand that a wrestler's "look" is a big part of her total package. At the risk of coming across as a feminazi, I also understand that a woman's looks are generally her most important asset in public life, and the dominant opinion is that a big rack is definitely hot.

I could live with being a heel because I'm usually bigger, tougher-looking, and not as cute (at least by mainstream standards) as many of my opponents, but to have a promoter wanting to fire me because my tits were too small was really just too much. James kind of reminded me of that "small-titted whore" kid from Pottsville, except Mr. St. Jean had no excuse because he is supposed to be all grown up. Maybe he wasn't breastfed as a baby or something, I don't know.

To make a long story short St. Jean wanted to fire me after that night. I think the whole thing bothered me because James had been very cordial and nice to my face, so I thought that he at least wanted me around. To hear this conversation took me totally by surprise and hurt my feelings. But life goes on and I turned and walked away, leaving James and Tony to their Battle of the Boobs.

I wandered around until I found my "manager," Rotten Robbie, sitting on the stairs. I was having a little trouble remembering exactly what I was supposed to do for my short introductory match. As you might imagine, I was feeling a bit anxious about actually getting in the ring and doing moves with another person for the first time in front of an audience. Plus, I was royally pissed off, which didn't help either. True, I wasn't exactly doing a whole lot but it was my first time. Fortunately Robbie was extremely patient with me and was happy to run over the script again and again. I was pacing up and down the hall trying to memorize what I had to do from a little notebook that I had brought with me, all the while trying to put the conversation I had overheard out of my mind. Finally, my time came so I strode back out and inter-rupted the announcer this time. I went through my "I Want a Match" rant yet again, which I ended by bouncing one of my elbow pads off the announcer's chest for emphasis.

I wasn't watching the entry ramp, but I could tell that my opponent — the girl I was in reality scheduled to wrestle —

was making her entrance because there was a nice pop from the crowd. I turned toward her as she slid into the ring, where she leg dived me and then started putting the boots to me while I was flat on my back. So I bailed out of the ring. (In truth I tripped on one of the camera cords in front of the commentary table that were inconveniently strewn about at ringside. Fortunately I have always been pretty good at falling in such a way that might not look pretty, but prevents me from getting hurt.) Meanwhile my opponent, whose name was Violet Flame, rolled out after me.

The referee was counting us both out, so I tried to roll back in the ring, but Flame yanked me out by the leg. Meanwhile Rotten Robbie got in her face, which gave me time to regroup and give Violet a forearm shot to the face. From there she and I traded punches and kicks as we brawled our way along ringside and towards the back. There was a table near the door, which led to one of the hallways outside of the main arena. So I grabbed Flame by the hair and introduced her face to Mr. Table. (At the time I was worried that I might have been a bit over-enthusiastic in my introductions but afterwards she told me it was fine.)

From there I grabbed her by the arm and dragged her through the doors into the back, where the other wrestlers were clustered around the television monitor. She and I sort of exploded into the midst of them and kept flailing away at one another, because some kids were watching from down the hall.

"Close the door!" Violet yelled as I hammered her head into one of those old fashioned radiators.

"Shit, somebody close the door or break us apart or something!" I said as I kicked Flame to the floor and picked up a fire extinguisher over my head like I was going to hit her with it. At that point several of the boys got the hint and got between us, "restraining" me from bashing her brains in while someone closed the door.

My performance was pretty horrible and to be honest I'm too embarrassed to go back and look at the footage. But it was my first time as a "wrestler" and Violet didn't complain. We both had a good laugh about the whole thing, and I got a nice hug from her husband, Steve, just before he went out and bodyslammed someone through the food concession window during his hardcore match. Nice guy, Steve, unless you want a hotdog.

The night wasn't over yet though. I went back down to the women's dressing room, opened the door and was about to walk in when I heard a male voice yell, "Jesus Christ, close the door!"

"Uh, sorry," I said as I froze in my tracks, then quickly backpedaled and closed the door. It was Tony Atlas's voice. I had no idea what was going on and I didn't really want to know. The whole thing was none of my business, and all I really wanted was to change, pack my bags, and go home. I was dead tired. Not so much from the match, but more from being nervous and on edge for three hours. My poor adrenal gland had gotten quite a workout that night and I was done in. So I plopped myself down in a chair outside the dressing room. The women's room was down a long side hall away from everyone else, so I was alone with my thoughts. As I ran through my experiences of the evening I heard Tony scream, "Ow, Jesus Christ!" followed by what sounded very much like whipping sounds.

I wasn't overly disturbed that Tony was apparently engaging in some sort of S&M session in the women's dressing room. I had been warned that professional wrestling could be a little unusual. What disturbed me was that they were using my whip and doing God knows what with my handcuffs. I toyed with the idea of knocking again, but decided to go watch the rest of the show instead and hope that Tony and whoever was in there with him would clean my stuff off when they were done with it.

CHAPTER NINE

"DON'T BE AFRAID TO BE A LITTLE STIFF WITH THE PUNCH"

STORMDATE: January, 1999.

I was on my first roll. I had been featured as a wrestler on a live show, and had apparently narrowly avoided being fired because of certain anatomical irregularities. And less than a week had gone by when I received an e-mail from a guy named Bill, who told me that he was the booker for Hardcore Wrestling near Cleveland. Bill said that a friend of mine had told him about me and he was interested in bringing me out to shoot an angle in his next show.

The friend in question was Leann Runner, whom I had met over the Internet through a forum called the women's wrestling mailing list. She and I had a lot in common. We were both near the beginning of our training as wrestlers, we both loved the "sport," and we both had new Web sites. She was billing herself as Rageina Cage and was going to be a valet at the upcoming Hardcore Wrestling show. I was looking forward to working with her and eventually getting in the ring as one of her opponents when we both had a little more experience.

So I made the flight out to Cleveland, and rented a car at the airport. From there I rendezvoused with a freelance writer by the name of Jim Gerard. Jim had seen my Web site and wanted to do an article about me for *Penthouse* magazine. We had several telephone conversations where I gave him some background information and told him some personal things that might be useful for a story. Based on our discussions, he decided that he would chronicle my attempts to break into professional wrestling and find a wrestling school. To this end he had come to Ohio to follow me around and write about what happened.

We followed the directions Bill gave us to the Motel Six where we were staying, and I only got moderately lost once. As promoter-inspired directions go Bill's were pretty good. I think that Jim found my driving a little "creative," but he didn't openly complain (unless you count the times his knuckles turned white because he was clutching the emergency brake handle).

But as fate would have it we arrived at the Motel Six in one piece and checked in. Bill was staying in the room adjoining mine. They were rooming me with Leann, and she had already arrived and left her luggage. She had filled the sink with ice and was cooling down a six-pack of Budweiser and a couple of Diet Cokes. She had left a note that said, "Help yourself, Amanda," which to date has been the only time someone I've roomed with has done anything like that.

Bill came over and introduced himself and told me that if I wanted to take part in the autograph signing at a record store then I needed to be ready in five minutes. So I threw a few things into a bag, and we followed Bill to the store. Things were pretty much in full swing when we arrived. I could see that I was going to fit right in with this crowd. There were a number of wrestlers sitting at a table signing autographs, including Rageina. At an adjoining table were a group of men dressed in latex suits that made them look kind of like naked mutant cyborgs. It was, of course, the band GWAR. I don't remember their names, but my favorite one was the small, blonde guy who had a giant wrench in place of his arm.

I shook hands with each of the wrestlers and quietly introduced myself when they weren't busy with the fans. Then I pulled up a chair and started chatting with people as they came by, did a little flexing, and even signed a couple of autographs myself. Naturally I turned to a Hispanic guy who was wearing a Superman T-shirt and said in a loud voice, "You know, I have bigger arms than anyone at this table. I bet I could take all of you arm wrestling at once." (Actually three of the four guys were far more powerful-looking than I was but I find you can get a lot of mileage with the fans by saying things that are patently ridiculous.)

Oddly enough Rageina almost fell out of her seat in her rush to take up the Amanda Storm Challenge. This surprised me because unless looks were deceiving I was quite a bit stronger than Rageina.

"Are you sure?" I asked her quietly.

"Put up or shut up," she said in a loud voice.

What could I do? I put my arm up on the table.

"I'm not going to let you win, you know, with all of these people watching," I whispered and gave her a little smile.

Leann had this almost elfin sparkle in her eye as she plopped her arm up on the table. The guy in the Superman shirt pulled his chair back and frowned a little. The fans clustered around the table suddenly grew quiet. Now here was a woman with a competitive spirit who couldn't be daunted even in the face of defeat. She definitely had the heart of a pro wrestler.

"You had better not let me win," Leann whispered back, "because I'm going to whip your ass."

Damn, I liked this girl.

If this had been a made-for-television movie or a pro-wrestling angle, Leann would have probably won after a hard battle or I would have dumped the table on her like Jackie did to Sable on RAW once, setting up something for the pay-per-view or at least the show in Elyria the next day. But this was real life, and I beat her in less than a second. It felt kind of anti-climactic but I didn't let my feelings show. I just winked at her and smiled surreptitiously.

"Superman" leaned over to his buddy and said something about yours truly in Spanish that wasn't very nice. I didn't take it personally because I've noticed that some of the smaller male wrestlers don't like being around women who curl more than they do. Normally I wouldn't have singled out anyone or if I did I would have gone after the biggest monster in the place in an effort to be funny. But "Superman" had it coming.

"How about you, Superman?" I sneered. He just held up his hands and insulted me again in Spanish. I just laughed like I didn't understand, but actually my comprehension of Spanish and a couple of other languages is reasonably good. Sometimes I have found that you can learn a lot about people by making believe you can't understand them. I guess my secret is out now though, at least for people who read this book.

I didn't see anything to be gained by continuing this line of conversation. The whole arm wrestling thing was supposed to be a joke. I didn't actually expect anyone to take me up on it. So I wandered off and started chatting with some Goth girls who had come with their boyfriends to see GWAR. Naturally they had no clue who I was but they thought that my whips were cool, and I in turn admired their body piercings.

I really had no idea who GWAR was until I talked to some of their fans. Apparently they are a band who has been on the verge of making it big for some time now, but as I understand are a bit too extreme for the mainstream. They are big wrestling fans though, and one of the boys told me that they made their own fake vomit, blood, and feces as well as the latex mutant costumes they all wore. I was deeply impressed.

Meanwhile Jim Gerard was standing in the background finding everything a bit strange — if his facial expression was any clue — and with good reason. At that point, I hadn't even engaged in professional wrestling in any real way, yet it had taken me down a strange path already. I was standing in a

This is why I'm nice to my chiropractor
MIKE HOLMES

record store in Ohio having a very reasonable conversation about fake blood with a man wearing nothing but a latex costume that made him look like a naked mutant cyborg with a giant wrench for an arm.

The autograph signing was fun, though there was one incident that got a little ugly. One guy started to get a little obnoxious towards one of the wrestlers. He was infected by that species of courage that comes from being half in the bag. I just happened to be standing behind the wrestler in question and I thought that the whole thing was a work. So I started in too.

"Hey, tough guy. You fight one bean you fight the whole burrito. *Tu comprende, Cabron?*" I couldn't resist throwing that in for Superman, who was sitting at one of the tables to the side watching the proceedings.

"Yeah, I'll kick your ass and my girlfriend will kick your girlfriend's ass!" was his reply. Actually he said quite a bit more than that, but nine of the 10 words aren't ones I'm willing to put in my book. His girlfriend, who wasn't drunk, was pulling at the guy's arm trying to drag him out of the store.

"Don't worry about me, hon, but thanks. You've got balls," the wrestler said to me quietly as he stood in the door. I don't remember his name but I do remember that he pretty much filled the doorway.

"Sorry, I thought it was all part of the show."

My new wrestler "boyfriend" turned and chuckled a little.

"You haven't been doing this long have you?"

"Um, no, not really. Sorry if I got in the way."

"Don't worry about it, hon."

From there we were about to strike up a nice conversation that probably would have included copious restaurant tips when a group of fans came up and asked for his autograph. Apparently he was one of the regular heavyweights who had a local following. I was feeling a little out of sorts and embarrassed so I seized the moment and slipped away into the back. I had heard through the grapevine that there were free sandwiches and soda. I hadn't eaten since the flight and I wanted to live cheaply, since as King Kong Bundy likes to say, "We aren't here to spend money."

The rest of the session was pretty anti-climactic, so Jim and I went back to the motel. The party was in full swing in the promoter's room on the other side of the wall, and it wasn't long before Rageina had come back with a bunch of wrestlers in tow. We ended up sitting around talking about wrestling (what else?) and I have to admit that I found it a little amusing watching two guys trying to powerbomb each other on the floor between the beds.

"Save it for the show," one of the veteran guys yelled.

I just laughed and pulled a soda out of the sink and stood up against the wall with Jim.

"Pretty interesting bunch of people, huh, Jim?"

"I have to admit that this isn't quite what I expected," he replied.

It wasn't quite what I expected either, though I didn't really have too many preconceptions. But I wasn't expecting our room to turn into a cross between *Animal House* and *Wrestlemania XIV.* The other thing that caught me off guard was that I seemed to be the only person who didn't smoke or drink. I found this to be the case that first time I was in Pottsville, and apparently living hard was the norm for a lot of guys on the road.

A couple of the guys noticed the "toys" in my open suitcase: the whips, handcuffs, leather bondage wear, and so on. I have since wised up and now I don't leave my things out in the open before a show, but it wasn't long before the guys were hitting each other with my whips and in general getting a little too enthusiastic. Urgh. I told everyone that I was going over to the party next door, so I could have an excuse to make the boys stop playing with my toys without coming across like a spoil sport.

"Mind if I tag along?" Jim whispered.

"Of course not. That's why you're here, right?"

With that we made our way over to Bill's room. I was beginning to wonder how many people were on this show because there had to be at least 20 guys partying it up in his room. As it turned out, not all of the guys were actually wrestlers on the show. Some were friends of wrestlers, ring crew, and the various other support people that help put together or at least hang around indie shows.

I was a little nervous, being the only woman in the room and all. But I sat around and did my best to laugh and joke and just be "one of the boys." I have since become very good at putting on this face but this was really the first time I had tried to take on that particular role. My reasoning was that I had basically two paths I could go down if I wanted to get a lot of bookings and in general work a lot on professional wrestling shows: I could sleep around with promoters, book-ers, and influential wrestlers. This I simply would never do. I have far too much respect for myself to sleep my way onto something as trivial as a wrestling show, or anything else for that matter. Plus I am married and love my husband. The other avenue was to basically act like one of the guys. Make the same jokes, act really comfortable around them, and try to infiltrate my way into their "space" by basically being one of them in everything but an anatomical sense. So this is what I did and it seemed to work. But I wasn't very experienced at playing this game and I made a bit of a miscalculation.

"Hey, do you have that outfit from your Web site?" one of the guys asked.

"Yeah, I sure do. I'm going to wear it tomorrow."

"How about trying it on now?" Bill asked. "I'd like to take some pictures of you with our belt." Bill showed me this rather cheap-looking "Heavyweight Champion" belt that had been making the rounds amongst the boys. I don't think it was one of the horrible WCW replica belts but it was pretty close.

"Sure! I'll be back in about 10 minutes." For some reason I thought that Bill mentioned he was going to put them up on his Web site. So I went back and got into my outfit. I was planning on appearing in front of a crowd tomorrow wearing the thing, and it certainly was risqué. And I didn't do anything that I had cause to be ashamed of. I simply hit a few muscle poses and let Bill take some pictures with the belt. Even so, now that I know a little more about how the game is played, I wouldn't do it again because I instantly destroyed what I had just built up. By showing off my outfit before the show, some of the boys started to think of me as female. I know this sounds strange but bear with me.

Of course the boys are going to think of me as a woman. I wouldn't have it any other way. But a woman can hang out with a group of men in a way that a female can't. When a group of men start thinking of Amanda as a female then I end up getting into these types of conversations:

"So, how do you like being on the road?" Dirty Dick asks, as he puts his arm around my shoulders.

I block the hip toss. She counters by breaking into opera
MIKE HOLMES

"Um, fine. Can't complain." I gently remove his arm. He chuckles a bit. It obviously excites him that I'm playing a little hard to get.

"I like travelling because you can do what you want. Do you get to do what you want?" He puts his arm around me again.

"Yes, but I'm married."

"But what he doesn't know won't hurt him, right?" At that point I usually start feigning menstrual cramps and go hide in the women's bathroom or something. Since I've learned how to play the game, I make it a point not to show up at events in nice dresses or all dolled up, at least not until I'm an established worker for a particular promotion. And I most definitely do not model my outfits for the boys. Well, at least not in the way that I did at Elyria.

I left Bill's room soon afterwards, because I felt very uncomfortable. I went back to my room, changed back into street clothes, and got a little sleep. I was starting to feel the jet lag and I wasn't really used to travelling yet. After about half an hour, Leann came back with some of the boys but I didn't really want to talk or socialize so I pretended that they hadn't woken me up. As it turned out, I had the room to myself for the rest of the night. I suspect that Jim Gerard and I were the only people associated with Hardcore Wrestling who didn't completely party the night away. By the looks of some of the workers the next morning, my suspicions were indeed confirmed. But such is life when you travel with the circus.

The next morning after a breakfast of cereal and skim milk at Denny's, Jim and I went over to the conference center that, on that day, was the Hardcore Wrestling Arena. I sat around and watched the ring crew and other support people perform all of the little and not so little tasks that go into getting ready for an independent show. Jim and I talked, and he floated around asking some of the other performers questions. Once the ring was set up I jumped in to "test" it out.

I was one of those people like in Pottsville now. I knew just enough to show off, but not quite enough to save it for the show. Besides, I wanted to show Jim that I knew how to do some moves. It couldn't hurt, right? Well, I had just recently started practicing vaulting over the top rope to the floor from a standing position. So I grabbed the top rope with both hands, just like I had been shown in wrestling school. I looked out of the corner of my eye and made sure Jim was watching. He was. I leapt up and over the top rope, and made it, but just barely. The fly in the ointment was I lost my footing as soon as I hit the floor and landed right on my fat butt. Ouch. I hadn't counted on the tile being slippery. Plus I didn't have actual wrestling boots yet. I was still making do with some biker boots that I had bought from a Sacramento-area Harley shop back in my biker-mama days. One thing about a good set of wrestling boots is that they offer a fairly reasonable amount of traction on a variety of surfaces. The boots I was wearing, on the other hand, were designed mainly to look cool. (Fortunately, the only thing that was truly injured was my pride.)

The match itself was one of those contests you generally only see in states that don't have an athletic commission. The main protagonist was a rather mellow young man named Chris, whose ring name was "The Wifebeater." His valet for the evening was Rageina. I forget who Chris's opponent was, even though I carried the guy's business card around in my luggage for six months. I think his first name was Logan.

The match was a combination of brawling, aerial maneuvers, and broken furniture. Rageina's job was to follow Wifebeater around during his match. Periodically Beater would turn his attention away from his opponent to threaten and manhandle Rageina, which the crowd didn't seem to appreciate. About halfway through the contest I came out to watch. The crowd responded to me instantly, comparing me to Chyna. I walked around the ring stepping on tacks so they would stick in the soles of my boot. The match before ours had involved thumbtacks being dumped outside the ring and I was worried about someone getting hurt. Chris and Logan were doing a lot of bumping outside the ring and I wanted to help them if I could.

Towards the end of the match, Wifebeater had beaten down his opponent and turned to Rageina. He didn't like how she had acted during his match and started really pushing her around. That was my cue. I turned my attention to them and acted like I didn't approve of what was going on in the slightest. (This didn't take much acting ability on my part.) Then Beater grabbed a chair and made like he was going to hit Rageina with it. That was when I jumped into the ring, spun him around, punched him in the jaw, and started working him over. He quickly got over on me by raking my eyes and then he punched me in the mouth. Hard. Then he hit me over the head with a chair. Hard. I'm not sure how the match ended, because I was lying in the middle of the ring pretending that I was knocked out. I think that Logan won, though my memory fails me.

I made a lot of mistakes that weekend, and I think some of them stemmed from thinking that I knew more about wrestling than I really did. Chris and I were going over what we were going to do before our match. The last thing I wanted was for Wifebeater to give me some really fake-looking punch because he didn't want to hurt me. I had this experience with some of the guys in my training and I didn't want it to happen in front of a live crowd.

"Don't be afraid to be a little stiff with the punch," I told him.

"Are you sure?"

"Yeah. That's how I want it."

What I should have done was just let Chris worry about making himself look good and trust him to use proper professional judgment. Either that or have him give me a punch while we were talking, which would have been an even better idea. Instead, I thought that I knew more than I did and used the word "stiff" where I should have said "tight." There is a world of difference between the two. A lot of people "work a little tight." This means that they perform moves in a rugged fashion that is designed to look good but they still protect their opponent. Stiff just means that it hurts. So what I basically said to Chris was, "Don't be afraid to punch me in the jaw." And he was a good man because he did exactly what I asked.

Once the match was over Rageina helped me to my feet. I grabbed the microphone and challenged Wifebeater to a match later in the show. This was my first time talking in the ring and I was terrified.

"Wifebeater, are you man enough to accept the Amanda Storm challenge?" He looked amused. I would too if I had just punched someone in the jaw and hit them over the head with a chair.

"How about this? You get in the ring with me and we'll rock and roll." My heart was pounding and as I paused I wasn't sure what to say next. I bent over and picked up the chair Chris had conveniently left for me in the middle of the ring. As I picked up the chair I remembered what I was supposed to say: "How about this? You think are so tough beating up poor Rageina. How about later tonight you get in the ring with Amanda Storm and we'll have a no-DQ chair match?"

With that I threw the chair at Wifebeater, where he was standing outside the ring. That was a bit of improv, but what with barbed wire, thumbtack, and light bulb matches I didn't think that the promoter would mind. Fortunately my opponent was standing outside the immediate proximity of the fans. With that I left the ring and made my way to the back as Wifebeater retreated into the locker room.

Sadly the match never took place. Apparently the building manager was a little disturbed by the fact that the wrestlers were destroying all of his tables and tearing up the place in general. The match before ours was the sort of hardcore match that gives professional wrestling a bad name. Bill and Hardcore Wrestling were very nice to me and they are great guys, but here you have two guys battling in a ring where there are 7-foot long fluorescent lightbulbs in the corners, barbed wire around the ring, and of course, a couple buckets full of thumbtacks in and around ring. Something tells me this isn't what the manager was anticipating when he decided to allow wrestling in his building. So he canceled the rest of the show, which unfortunately included my match.

After the show, one of the wrestlers in the match was talking to Jim. The guy had a sliver of glass in his eye from being hurled into one of the lightbulbs. He didn't seem overly concerned about it when Jim asked him about it.

"Oh, it's just a piece of glass. It'll come out."

The mind reels.

We left soon after and haven't seen that guy since. Hell, I don't even remember his name but I hope he didn't lose his eye. I suppose if things didn't work out he could also change his wrestling name to "Long John" and do a pirate gimmick. (His finisher could be called "making him walk the plank" or "sending him to Davy Jones's locker." Naturally it would have to be something off the top rope though, which might be a bit hard for someone with only one eye.)

Jim seemed satisfied with the material he got for the *Penthouse* article, though apparently the promoter didn't give him quite the backstage access that he was promised. But Jim was going to come to another of my matches in a couple of months, a match in Concord, New Hampshire that was bigger than I or I think anyone on the card could have imagined. . . .

You know, that would have been a great place to end this chapter, but there is a postscript to all of this. About a year later, I had all but forgotten about this match when a friend of mine handed me a copy of *Wrestling Superstars*. On page 22 was the following: "Amanda Storm, standing tall for women everywhere, has declared war on the Beater." A pity the match never took place. On the other hand, in retrospect it was probably just as well because I really did need more training and experience. Fortunately the next week I would be back at Kowalski's getting more of both.

CHAPTER TEN

WEIRDOPALOOZA.COM

I did an interview for the Weirdopalooza Web site not long after the Ohio match. I have done a lot of interviews in my first year as a wrestler, but this was my first *real* interview. (Not counting Jim Gerard of course.) I highly recommend the site, though I think parents might find it to be somewhat on the R-rated side. Robert, or "Liquorhead" as he likes to be called, combines a charmingly warped sense of humor with a love of wrestling and a facility with software to produce one of the funniest wrestling Web sites I have seen to date.

The best thing that was ever on Weirdopalooza was me, but then, I may be a little biased. I have edited the interview a bit, but I tried to preserve the spirit of the piece as it appeared on the site.

Q: What's the most bizarre foreign object you've ever had to use in the ring?

A: I never have *had* to use a foreign object in my life. But probably one of the more bizarre objects I have used in a match (and I'm not making this up) is a rubber chicken. A fan threw it into a ring when I was being beaten down by two male heel wrestlers. I was supposed to make a comeback and throw them both out of the ring when they started arguing after I was out, so I beat both of them with the chicken and chased them to the locker room, where all three of us almost died from fits of laughter. I thought that one of the wrestlers was playing a joke but it turned out that the whole thing was totally unplanned. The fan who threw it asked me for it back after the show, and naturally I autographed it.

Q: If you were a cartoon dog, do you think you could kick Hong Kong Phooey's ass in a shoot fight?

A: It would be a tough fight, but I think that Amanda Storm would have the edge. HK's ground skills seem to be weak and that is where I excel. Plus I've had enough boxing practice that I could probably hold my own with him on my feet. But the critical thing is that Hong Kong seems to have rather frequent runs of bad luck. So I would probably end up just standing there and watch him trip over a banana peel and put his head through a brick wall.

Q: What would you say your animal spirit guide is?

A: I'm not entirely sold on the idea of "animal spirit guides." But if someone asked me that question over beer and pretzels, I would have to say the black widow spider. I don't so much think of myself as being like a black widow, but I did have a dream once in which a black widow figured prominently. She came to me out of darkness first as a searing hourglass. Finally, as she neared, her bloated form revealed much that was once merely darkness.

"Obey my voice, young Demon. I am God from Eternity to Eternity," Black Widow said. Her voice was pregnant with crystalline hatred. Before I could ask her if she and William Blake were buds, a strangeness came over me. I reeled as my brain shivered and expanded, then contracted like a dying star. My cortex shivered as it transmuted into a dense, chitinous lump of echopractic tar. My neurons ceased to fire with the rhythms of animal life and instead pulsed to the irresistible droning beat of insectile consciousness. . . .

Happily, I awoke just in the nick of time. The only logical conclusion I could form from such a dream was that Black Widow wanted me to become a professional wrestler. So I did. Such is the calculus of my daydreams.

Q: Do you prefer camping in a tent, or just open air in a sleeping bag?

Make a wish!
MIKE HOLMES

A: I don't go camping because in truth I get enough of that when I'm on the road for wrestling shows. I have slept in my car more than once, a highway underpass once, and a culvert twice. But if I did go camping I would probably have two of my slaves carry my eight-woman tent on their backs. Naturally, I'd need the room for my toys and other creature comforts. Television, portable fridge, stereo system, that sort of thing. The boys would sleep outside of course. And if they were both very good and very lucky I might let them have sleeping bags.

Q: If you met someone who was your soul mate, and they asked you to stop wrestling, would you?

A: If the guy was my "soul mate" then he wouldn't ask me to stop wrestling. The reason for this is simple. I am a somewhat dominant woman and for me to really connect with a man, he has to become my "humble and obedient servant." In other words, his world must revolve around me, Me, ME. His every waking effort and thought must go toward making me comfortable. If you think that is too much to ask then you couldn't possibly be my soul mate. Does that answer your question?

Q: What wrestler deserves to be on a postage stamp?

A: A lot of wrestlers deserve this honor, but none more so than George "The Animal" Steele. Surely his green tongue and many years of eating turnbuckles should count for something? He has truly served as a worthy role model and inspiration for two generations of this nation's youth. It brings a tear to my eye to think that Mr. Steele is not getting the accolades he deserves in his dotage.

Q: What was your favorite lunch box you had as a child?

A: I would have to say it is a toss-up between Barbie and Wonder Woman. Believe it or not I still have the Barbie one. Maybe I should take it to shows and use it as a foreign object? Actually, ironically enough it is in pretty good shape so it would probably be too valuable to wrap around some guy's head in a wrestling show.

Q: Is there a wrestling move you're too afraid to do?

A: No, not really. There are plenty of wrestling moves that I don't know *how* to do, but none that I'm actually afraid to try and learn. My "style," if you can call it that, is somewhat "old-school" because that is where my trainers are coming from. I can do some of the newer moves and of course I'm more than willing to truck out one of the newer goofy WWF-style moves for cheat heat, but isn't everyone?

Q: Have you ever wrestled a guy and have him grab you inappropriately?

A: What is "inappropriate" in a sport where the rules are considered by the vast majority to be more akin to guidelines? Actually I'm probably the one who is doing the majority of the "inappropriate grabbing." Why do you think I prefer to wrestle men to women? Not too long ago I wrestled a guy named Matt Storm (no relation, mercifully) and my counter to his leg drop was to literally bite him between the legs. You can bet that the crowd loved that one more than Matt did.

Q: A battle royale with Chyna, Sable, Sunny, Jackie, Luna, Koko B. Ware, Doink, and Amanda Storm . . . describe what you would do to win.

A: This is a tough one. Well, Chyna went to the same wrestling school that I'm going to, so I'd probably start out by teaming up with her and tossing Koko B. Ware out of the ring, along with his little dog Toto. (Or did he have a bird? I forget.) Chyna and I would then probably stand in the corner and exchange restaurant tips while Sable and Luna beat the crap out of each other. So we can scratch those two off the list. By the time they were out of the ring, both women would have ripped off each other's clothes and Luna would be beating Sable into semi-consciousness with her ubiquitous leather strap, or maybe the other way around.

I'd tell Chyna to take care of Doink while I went after Sunny (I'm not stupid), and to be honest I think that Doink would probably get rid of Chyna by threatening to do a striptease in the ring. Chyna would probably eliminate herself and flee screaming back to the dressing room. (Given the people that are playing Doink lately, I know that I would too.) Meanwhile, while the clown was occupied, I'd schoolboy him and give him my Matt Storm finishing move. Then I'd blade myself and chase Sunny around the ring with a pole axe that happened to be conveniently laying at ringside. Since Sunny is essentially a valet, I think this would probably take her out of the running.

Then I'd bleed all over Doink's face and then smear his face paint so he couldn't see. If I were feeling especially frisky, I might pickpocket his eyeballs. Then, after performing unauthorized root canal surgery, I would gorilla press him and heave him into the third row for the 1-2-3. Got Milk?

Q: If you had to wear a mask, what would it look like?

A: I think that it would be cool to wear a mask that looks exactly like my normal face so no one could tell I was wearing a mask. Then during the match I would wow the crowd with my incredible strength. After I got the pin I would pull off the mask, revealing one of my secrets to all and sundry. The mask hides a network of wires and electronics! Amanda Storm is in actuality an android like in that old episode of *The Six Million Dollar Man*! (And you thought that I was just another pretty face.)

Actually in truth I do wrestle under a hood sometimes. The mask is black with a silver eagle, and black mesh so you can't see any part of my face under the holes. I do this in shows where the building owner "doesn't want girls" or if the promoter is too cheap to hire another woman to have a match but still wants me to wrestle on his show but doesn't want to promote a man vs. woman match. So that is when the "Midnight Assassin" comes crawling out from the rock "he" hides under and does his thing, which usually involves losing.

Q: If Vince McMahon offered you a job if you would get Triple-E implants, would you do it?

A: Only if he got them first. Actually I think it might be cool. I could change my name to "Flotation Device Girl" and as well as wrestle, I could moonlight as a lifeguard. Do you think I'd get a cameo on *Baywatch*?

Q: Do you know "the secret"?

*A Kuwaiti oil baron? Sadly,
I found out later he was
from Jersey*
SUSAN WHITNEY

A: I know lots of secrets, including "The Secret." There is a secret society we wrestlers belong to. Special handshakes, discounts on auto insurance, restaurant tips, the whole nine yards. (And you thought when wrestlers talk about "ruling the world" it was all just a work.) If you know "The Secret" then you know what I mean. The horror writer, H.P. Lovecraft knew "The Secret" when he wrote that we all must be "on guard against a specific, lurking peril which, though it will never engulf the whole race, may impose monstrous and unguesseable horrors upon certain venturesome members of it." Think about it . . . we're the same you and I. We're the same!

Q: Would you party in the Horseman's Lear jet?

A: Only if Chris Benoit agreed to trade chops with me.

139

Q: What does your family think of your profession?

A: My family thinks I'm a lunatic, given that I spent a number of years in college getting several rigorous but essentially meaningless degrees. Yes, I know two languages besides English and no one speaks either of them anymore, at least outside of the Roman Catholic and Greek Orthodox Churches. I love my family, but mom and dad aren't paying my student loans, so I figure that my choices are my own. I always, as a point of honor, take the "path less traveled."

Q: Ever had someone come on to you at a wrestling event?

A: Oh god, I have never *not* had someone come on to me at a wrestling event. Men, women, whatever, I've seen it all. Strangely, I never really thought of myself as a sex symbol. I have always tried to leave that for the valets and the women wrestlers who are comfortable in that role. But you can't always control what people think, though that has never stopped me from trying.

Q: What's your favorite entrance theme?

A: I don't really have a favorite theme, but I do have a tendency to use a song for awhile until I get bored with it and move on to something else. I started out with "Celebrity Skin" by Hole. I have used "Gor Gor" by GWAR quite a bit, and currently I'm using "Bled for Days" by Static-X a lot. This song has the advantage of working well for me as a babyface in my mixed matches. When I'm a babyface in women's matches, which used to be never but is happening more and more often now, I just tell the promoter, "Put on something that sounds friendly."

Q: Do you ever drive with your arm hanging out the window and curl the air up and down with your fingers?

A: What kind of question is that? No offense, but I think you need to beat someone in your interview department to death with a rubber statuette of Nixon for asking me that one! But to answer your question, "No."

Q: How do you explain the sexual allure of Mark Henry?

A: I'm not really sure why men find Mark Henry attractive. He does dress nice and though I have never met the man, I'll bet he smells like cloves. Maybe that is it. Guys like a man who smells like cloves? So far as women are concerned, I think that we find Mark attractive because he is attainable. I mean if he'll go out with Mae Young, then he will probably go out with 90% of the women who watch wrestling, and you probably couldn't say that about, say, Steve Blackman (yum) or Edge.

Q: What's your ultimate career fantasy match?

A: Going twenty minutes with HHH and then having him pedigree me and pin me with his feet on the ropes. He walks back to the dressing room but the referee calls him back, we continue the match and I hit him with the championship belt, pedigree him and strip him of the WWF women's title. Book me, Vince!

Q: Does Captain Crunch rip up the roof of your mouth when you eat it?

A: I don't eat that kind of stuff. I only eat healthy food to maintain my bodybuilder physique. Pizza, chips, soda, candy bars, that sort of thing. I'm very strict, you see.

CHAPTER ELEVEN

"I TOLD YOU IT WOULD HURT!"

STORMDATE: March 23, 1999.

It had been two months since my first wrestling match. One good thing about a wrestler's first match is that it sort of breaks the ice. The first match is a hurdle that we all have to get over, and afterwards everything becomes a lot easier. It is a lot like being a virgin. Sure, the first time can be kind of scary but then, with practice, it becomes a lot more fun.

I was scheduled to wrestle Violet Flame in a return gig for the EWA at the Lewiston Armory. Unfortunately for me there was a giant snowstorm and my redoubtable opponent was stuck in Boston. So no wrestling match for poor Amanda. For real this time. These days I would probably suggest to the promoter that I wrestle one of the guys. But then it was a little different. I wasn't really comfortable wrestling in front of a crowd and I really only wanted to do it with Violet. I would have gotten in the ring with anyone the promoter wanted me to of course, but with Violet not available St. Jean didn't ask me to wrestle and I didn't volunteer. So it was back to being a valet again.

I teamed up with Rotten Robbie again, who was managing this guy whose real name is Cleon, and I don't have a clue as to his work name. One of Robbie's jobs was to let the fans know right from the beginning that the wrestler he was "managing" was a heel. Though, in this match the line between heel and babyface wasn't very clear. Cleon is one of those guys who has quite a bit of raw talent and a pretty good light-heavyweight physique. He also sports a tattoo of a black panther on his pec, which I thought was a nice touch. Nice guy too. At least he has always been cordial to me at the school, where we've done some spots together.

Unfortunately the match was pretty much a squash with some guy named "Natural Born Killer." Pretty original, huh? The basic pattern of the match was Cleon would do something to NBK, who would stand around and alternately look either amused or mildly irritated for a moment. Then Natural would do something extremely painful and nasty-looking to Cleon, who would fall down and roll around in his own vomit for awhile. This lasted for about two minutes until NBK and Cleon took pity on the fans, and put an end to the whole sorry business.

Actually Cleon worked hard in the ring and did a nice job of making Natural look invincible. Personally I think that squash matches are a waste of the fan's time. I remember back in the 1980s when that was all they used to show on the WWF outside of the pay-per-views. And you know what, I hardly ever tuned in. I'd try to watch but after 10 minutes I'd start chanting, "Boring! Boring!" and turn it over to *The Andy Griffith Show*. Even so, it takes just as much if not more skill to take an ass-kicking as it does to give one. It also takes the willingness to put your ego aside. The attitude of most fans is pretty much in line with how things are in America — we love a winner. I've both won and lost my share of matches and one thing that I have noticed is that my picture and merchandise sales increase dramatically when I win as opposed to lose. And this is true whether I'm a heel or a babyface. People quite simply like to identify with a winner, whether she wears black or white.

Having said all of this, the fans really aren't the most important people a wrestler needs to impress. True, it is important that we give the people a good show, but the respect of your fellow wrestlers is extremely important, and they generally respect people who are good entertainers. They don't base their good opinions on who wins or loses. In fact, most of the time we are in the back and really have no idea who is going over in any given match.

More importantly, if a promoter asks a wrestler to go out and take a beating and she does it well, the fans may not be impressed but the promoter will be happy and might very well want her on future shows. This has happened to me more than once. I go up and do a job for a local "star" and give it my all. Win or lose it doesn't matter. Then a month later the promoter will call me back and this time I might lose again, but at least I'm still on the show. Then a funny thing happens. Amanda starts winning a few matches. And before you know it she is winning more than she loses, and is even finding her way onto the posters.

I had a conversation with Jacques Rougeau a while back when he was outlining how he wanted my performance to go in one of his shows. I had made the drive up to Montreal before and put over one of his girls, but this time he was giving me the push of my life in front of over 3,000 people. I couldn't believe it. I tried to keep a straight face but it was pretty obvious that I was excited.

"You're a good girl, Amanda, and I like your attitude," he said. "I think that you are one of those people who won't get a big head if you make it."

That was the philosophy Mike Hollow instilled in me right from the beginning, and I have tried my level best to live up to this ideal. Once I have been working for a promotion for a while I will certainly make suggestions if the booker is open to my ideas. But if the office wants a certain type of match, then I will do my best to give them that match. If I don't like how I am being used by a promotion in the long term, then I will try to get work with other companies and drop that particular group down from my A list to my B list. No hard feelings at all, and no bridges burned. But to tell you the truth, at this stage of my wrestling career all I really want is for people to know me.

Down I come off my old, moldy soapbox yet again and back to the show. I didn't really have much to do in that match other than, in NBK's words, "Stay out of the way, honey, and just do whatever." So that is what I did. I taunted the crowd, posed, threatened the cameramen, and accused several adolescent males of all sorts of things that I knew would make them mad. There was this one young man who kind of looked like a young Howdy Doody with an attitude, who almost came out of his chair and attacked me. Fortunately his older brother (they looked too much alike not to be related) held him back. That is one great thing about kids. They have big shiny buttons that are incredibly easy to push. I suspect that the kid was working me and was just showing off for the camera and maybe the other fans. I've done that myself a few times. "Hold me back! I'll kill him!" I have screamed more than once, while in reality having no intention of getting within a thousand miles of the guy. Makes for good comedy, though.

During intermission I came out and sold a few pictures. The EWA had tables set up for the wrestlers to come out to "meet and greet" the fans. All they asked was that we not sit next to our in-ring rivals and swap restaurant tips as the fans walked by. The crowd was good for an independent show — over 500 people — but they really weren't buying my stuff or anyone else's. The fans from Lewiston, Maine, were having fun, but they just didn't have a lot of extra money in their pokets. So I packed up my pictures and decided to make my own fun instead.

A local rock band called Twisted Roots was playing during intermission. They had a nice sound and their lead singer was sort of a poor man's David Lee Roth. So I jumped up on the stage and started doing my whirling dervish dominatrix impression, flailing my red and black flogger around like I was wielding a scimitar. I was standing directly behind the bass player, who was laughing as he played.

"Hit me in the back," he said.

"Are you sure?"

"Yeah. Give it to me, give it to me. Give it to me, baby."

"Uh, okie dokie."

So I wound up and really laid into him with the whip hard. It made a really sweet noise that elicited a few ooh's and ah's from the fans who were up against the stage in front of the mosh pit, watching the band. I was very pleased with the effect, all the more so because the whip was designed to have a far bigger bark than bite.

"Don't do that again!" the bass player squealed, as he danced around to try and cover up how much pain he was in. Boy, I'd hate to see the guy take a back bump or get hit with one of my whips that is actually supposed to hurt. I probably would have spent a night in the Androscoggin County Jail for manslaughter. (Then again, I'd hate to see me try to play a bass. Each according to her abilities, I suppose.)

I just laughed and went back to dancing. Once the song was over I perceived that my presence on the stage was no longer welcome. So I shook hands with the various members of the group, told the lead singer he was cute and jumped into a small mosh pit that had formed near the front of the stage. Big mistake. Poor Amanda Storm instantly became Mosh Target

This is truly what makes wrestling fun
FRANK WEST

Number One. I really should have expected this, but when it comes to having fun I can be a little impulsive sometimes.

So there I was surrounded by 13-year-old girls who were all literally hurling their little bodies at me. The leather corset was good armor and the girls mostly just bounced off me. It was really kind of cute. My biggest concern was more that they would hurt themselves and I would get the promoter and by extension myself in trouble. I could have done without this one kid who kept trying to kick me in the shins with his combat boots though. He tagged me with a good one right in the middle of my left shin. I howled in pain and was going to leave it at that. What could I do? If I wanted to dance, then I had to pay the fiddler.

"Haha. Storm ain't so tough. I kicked her ass," he said to

one of his little friends and everyone else within 10 feet. His buddy just kind of stood there looking nervous and not knowing what to do.

"Uh, dude, I don't think you should have done that," was his response.

The kids were still bouncing off me but I was basically ignoring them and staring at this kid. I didn't say anything, but my mind was racing. I wanted to figure out a way to make the boy realize that actions have consequences but at the same time do it Amanda Storm-style while not getting myself arrested for beating a minor to death. Plus if I was going to ever have a public "image" then I was going to learn how to deal with situations like this without getting myself thrown into jail or at least out of the show. I've been thrown out of public gatherings before and it is never pretty. I couldn't see myself, in my public role, going up to one of the police officers and complaining. They would have quite rightly pointed out that as a performer I probably should stay out of mosh pits.

"Is that your boyfriend, honey? He's kind of cute," I said to my assailant.

"Fuck you, bitch," was his pithy reply.

"Your girlfriend has a potty mouth," I said as I turned away, all the while watching the kid out of the corner of my eye.

The boy did exactly what I expected and charged me as soon as my back was turned. So I sidestepped at the last minute and right on cue he crashed into about three other people, who were busy throwing their bodies into each other. This made him the focal point of their attack and drew the heat off me. They weren't slightly afraid of him like they apparently were of me though, so these kids weren't shy about giving him feet and elbows and even head butts. I half expected someone to go for a power slam.

"My work is done here, I see," I said, half to myself. I decided that discretion was the better part of valor and quickly made my escape back to the autograph tables. Later my attacker's friend came up and asked for an autograph. There was no sign of his companion. Eaten by wolves, maybe?

Not all meetings with fans are so antagonistic. In fact, I met a fan once who left an impression on me I'll never forget. The strangest part is, she wasn't one of my fans. It was after a match I had in Fall River, Massachusetts. Many fans who enjoyed my performance were asking me for my autograph as I made my way out of the building.

A young man, probably a sophomore in college, came up to me as I was making my way toward the exit. The ring crew was busy tearing down the ring and packing up the chairs and barrier, while a few fans mingled and talked to some of the wrestlers.

"Excuse me, Chyna, would you sign my program?"

"Yeah, sure," I said, rolling my eyes a little. I don't think that I'm all that similar to Chyna, despite having gone to the same wrestling school and both being women. But when I'm a heel I sometimes play up the similarities by doing a lot more of HHH's moves than usual and working in a low blow or two. Then when the fans yell that I'm a "Chyna wanna-be"

I get mad and scream, "I'm not a Chyna wanna-be! I'm Amanda God-damn Storm and I'd destroy her or any other man, woman, or child who is stupid enough to step into the ring with me!" Right before the babyface would roll me up, of course. But that wasn't tonight.

"Have you been to these shows before?" I asked, figuring he might have seen me work as a heel. After all, I was wrestling in southeastern Massachusetts on almost a weekly basis and, much to my surprise and delight, some of the fans were starting to remember me.

"No, I saw your Web site and decided to come to the show and see you.

Wow, I was absolutely thrilled and more than a little surprised. I knew that more and more people were following my Web site, and I got a lot of e-mail from fans telling me that they enjoyed the accounts of my matches and my newsletter, but this was the first time a fan came up to me in person like this.

"I'm glad you like it. I hope you enjoyed the show."

"I did, yes. I was wondering if you could do me a favor?" I could tell he was nervous. My curiosity was piqued. The last guy who asked me for a favor and had a look on his face like this kid wanted me to do something that I won't even contemplate talking about in a book about professional wrestling.

"My sister thinks you're Chyna."

"Oh."

"Well, she is sick and the doctors say that she only has about three months. Her big dream has always been to meet Chyna. I don't think that is ever going to happen and I was wondering if you could go over to her and say a few words and say you're Chyna? It would really mean a lot to her . . . and me."

The guy looked like he was about to cry. This was *not* what I had expected him to ask. So I looked over and there was this girl, who couldn't have been more than five, in a wheelchair. By the looks of her she had cancer and was wearing an HHH T-shirt and had one of those green DX giant foam fingers. I walked over and knelt down beside her. The little girl's eyes lit up and she had a huge smile.

"Hi, honey, what's your name?" I asked softly.

"Jessica." Suddenly she was feeling shy and turned away.

"Do you know who I am?" I didn't want to say that I was Chyna just in case she knew I wasn't. That would be awkward for all of us and you can never really tell what kids know and what they don't, so I was playing it safe. In truth, my heart was breaking for this little girl who was fighting a horrible battle that she couldn't hope to win when she should be having the most carefree, happy-go-lucky years of her life. I know because many years ago I battled cancer myself and barely survived. I have two big scars across my chest as proof that I fought the hard fight, so I know how hard the big "C" can be. The difference was, I was a mature woman and this was a little girl.

"You're Chyna!" Jessica said, suddenly beaming again.

"I hear that you're my biggest fan. I'm lucky to have a friend like you," I said as I put my arms around her and gave her a hug.

"Are you and Hunter really married?" she asked.

"Oh yes," I said, laughing. "He's really sweet."

I answered a bunch of questions about what was going on in the World Wrestling Federation and I was lucky that I happened to be following the storyline lately, which isn't always the case when I'm busy. Finally I went over to the souvenir table (or the "gimmick table" as wrestlers like to call it) and rummaged through the pictures. The promotion sold pictures of all sorts of stars who never would set foot in their ring as well as wrestlers who had once in the past worked little indie shows like I was that night. Hulk Hogan, Undertaker, X Pac, Kevin Sullivan . . . I scrounged some more. Finally I hit paydirt and found a picture of HHH with Chyna standing in the background. She wasn't really that visible in the picture, but you could tell it was her. I signed it, "To my favorite friend in the whole world, Jessica. Chyna."

I haven't told anyone this story except for a few people I know on the Internet and my closest friends. I have to admit that I never expected to be seriously mistaken for Chyna and actually feel compelled to go along with the ruse. I left the venue with tears in my eyes and cried for an hour as I drove through the rain back to Maine. I was sad because I knew that sweet little girl wouldn't be in this world much longer and because the whole episode brought back horrible memories of my own that I had tried to bury some 10 years ago. But for one night I was the "Ninth Wonder of the World" and never again can I see that woman on my television set without thinking of Jessica.

"I TOLD YOU IT WOULD HURT!"

I think that our lives are defined by the good and bad we bring to the lives of others. There is a custom in some Buddhist countries for priests to beg, but in reality by asking you for food or money they are giving rather than receiving. For by giving you the opportunity to give them some trifle — a small coin or a crust of bread — the priests are offering the chance for their benefactor to build good karma, which are basically cosmic brownie points which you cash in to have a better life the next time around. So in truth Jessica was doing me as much a favor as anything I was doing for her, and I am very grateful that fate put her in my path and that "Chyna" was able to put a smile on her face for one night.

CHAPTER TWELVE

"YOU'RE LOOKING AT MY ASS, AREN'T YOU?"

STORMDATE: April 2, 1999.

I liked Dartmouth College the moment I rolled down my window and asked one of the students directions to Led Auditorium. "You're one of the wrestlers, aren't you?" the lad inquired after pointing at the huge building 50 feet to my right with "Led Auditorium" plastered all over it in big letters.

"Uh, yeah, thanks." I guess they still teach breeding at those Ivy League universities. If I had been back at good old Sacramento State, he probably would have said, "Can't you see the sign right in front of your face, you moron?" Or more likely he would have just ignored me and kept walking.

Tonight I was part of a six-wrestler tag bout, featuring four men and two women, my counterpart on the babyface side being Violet Flame. We had worked out a couple of spots in wrestling school since January and I was anxious to try them. The decision to put us in a tag match was a good one. Some wrestlers specialize in tag matches and as I found out in wrestling school there is definitely an art to such bouts. But when you see a six-man tag, the promoter is often throwing a bunch of wrestlers who lack experience or are new to the promotion in with a couple of "ring generals" and giving them some time in front of a crowd. This is especially useful if you want to include a couple of women wrestlers and have them mainly go after each other, which can be kind of problematic if you have a battle royale instead.

I met King Kong "Call Me Chris" Bundy while I was looking for a place in the dressing room to change. Technically it was a women's dressing room but for some reason they put all of the soda and beer on ice in a trash can with us. It is rare for promoters to provide cold drinks for their workers, and it is even rarer for the women to actually get any. (In this case, as it turned out, the drinks were courtesy of the college.) Usually if there are drinks, there are like 20 guys and two gals on the show, so if I want a cold one I have to invade the men's room or go thirsty. This was the first time I didn't have to bring my own refreshments, so I wasn't complaining. The only problem was that the guys basically took over our space to the point where we couldn't move around. So I wandered over to what was supposed to be the men's dressing room and changed in a stall. When I came out Dave Vicious was standing there totally naked.

"You're looking at my ass, aren't you?" Dave asked as he went about his business.

Geez, all I did was ask George how he got his tongue so green!
D.J. VON WYC

"Absolutely, Dave," I said, smirking a little.

The truth of the matter is that I wasn't really that interested in Dave's ass. You already know my stance on co-ed locker room situations, and besides — Dave wasn't really my type. I have always been a sucker for more of the sumo wrestler look. In all seriousness, men like Yokozuna and King Kong Bundy are the most gorgeous men on the planet as far as Amanda Storm is concerned, followed closely by certain defensive linemen. So in truth, I was discreetly checking out Chris, who was sitting on a bench off to the side with his trademark black singlet rolled down past his belly button. Now, dear readers, *that's* a man.

I was just going to get the drinks I came for and leave but Bundy smiled at me so I stuck around for a few minutes.

"Hi," King Kong said. "Call me Chris." Chris and I had a short but nice conversation and I went back to the women's side with two six-packs of soda in hand.

I've met Chris at a lot of shows since and it is always a real treat. I like him a lot and he is one of the few "stars" with whom I can actually sit down and have a nice conversation about something other than wrestling. I always greet him with a hug and a big, "Hello Mr. Bundy!" He always replies, "Call me Chris, Amanda!"

Actually since I've been in wrestling I've shared a locker room with quite a few people who you probably know if you have followed wrestling over the years. I sat beside George "The Animal" Steele once where we were both in our underwear changing for the show. I was talking to the guy I was

Jake said, "Damn, put those away. Your arms are bigger than mine!"
D.J. VON WYC

wrestling that night about hitting up a restaurant after the show. Neither of us knew the town so I turned to George.

"Have you ever been in this town before, Sir?" I asked.

"No, I'm sorry I haven't," he said and then he started laughing. "Wrestling sure has changed since my day!"

"Really? You mean it wasn't always like this?" I tried my best to look genuinely surprised.

I was supposed to valet a match for Jake Roberts in California but unfortunately things didn't work out and he wasn't able to wrestle. He showed up at the event and did a "personal appearance," which consisted of fans lining up to have their picture taken with him in the ring. That is the thing about wrestling. Don't count your money or get your hopes up about things until after they happen. Though, I did get a nifty picture with him, which was kind of fun. I enjoyed watching him on television with my grandfather, who would have gotten a kick if he could have seen the picture. (I don't know if he would have liked the leather outfit I wore, but you can't have everything.)

I had a nice conversation with Dan Severn in the corner of a junk room above a bar where I was booked on a show to wrestle a 270-pound monster whose last name was also Storm. (I'll tell you all about the match if there is a "second year" sequel to this little book.) Anyway, Dan asked me a lot of questions about how I liked wrestling and we both complained about how hard it was to make a decent living wrestling. The thing that struck me about Dan was that he was incredibly soft-spoken and polite. (Well, that and his gorgeous eyes.) He is also the only name guy who I have seen give out autographed pictures for free to all of the wrestlers who want one as a "professional courtesy," as he calls it. That is really nice, I think, because a lot of them will charge the young wrestlers who grew up watching them the same five bucks they charge the fans.

I've met other stars, but I usually don't say too much and try to give them their space. But I won't drop any more names now because I didn't meet most of them in my first year. So back to the match.

The evil side (we all wore black of course) was myself, Don Rotten, and Apocalypse. Don wore a shirt with a skeleton on the front that I thought was kind of neat, and he told me that it glowed in the dark. Apocalypse wore face paint and was one of those guys who liked headbutts. (You know the type.) On the opposing side were Violet, Freight Train, and Shane Williams.

We let the guys do their thing first. Wrestling events are 95% male-dominated so women wrestlers are something different, and it is always best to not open a match with dessert, if you know what I mean. I'm not trying to say that we were spectacular — far from it — but people were interested in seeing Violet and me wrestle.

The crowd was mostly college students, which, at a campus gym, is to be expected, but what surprised me was that probably half of the crowd were women. The other unexpected moment was when a group of about 10 students began "wrestling" right beside the ring during our performance. I happened to see it out of the corner of my eye and at first I thought it was a part of our match that I had managed to miss hearing about when Violet and I were talking over our spots beforehand.

"Are those guys down there part of the show?" I asked Don. I made a motion in the ring to make it appear that I was talking about the match.

He looked down at them for a second and thought about it.

"Could be, but I don't think so."

I looked more closely and indeed Don was right. They were basically a bunch of college students who decided to have their own little match right then and there. One of them even hit his friend in the head with a chair. I guess that is what you get for running a wrestling show at a college without any security.

Apocalypse and Rotten pretty much threw Shane around for awhile and he tagged out to Violet, so that was my cue to come in. We locked up and ran through some simple spots that she and I had practiced at Kowalski's. I took Flame to the ropes, gave her a knee to the gut, shot her off for a clothesline, and then gave her some kicks. Hardly inspiring stuff, but it was light years better than it had been in January. My kicks were still pretty awful though, mainly because I still needed a lot of practice and I was afraid of hurting Violet. At the risk of sounding like I'm blowing my own horn, I'm pretty proud of my kicks now and I have spent a lot of time getting yelled at by Mike Hollow and practicing abusing the middle turnbuckle. The trick is to make the kicks look real while not hurting the person. There are a lot of wrestlers, especially the newer ones, who say, "They're stiff because I want them to look good." What they really should say is, "They're stiff because I'm not good enough to do them right." At the time I preferred my kicks to look a little weak to laying them in on someone I out-weighed by 50 pounds. But I was also dedicated to improving and it was my goal to make each match better than the last.

Then I turned away from Violet and started posing and flexing for the crowd. This has since become one of my trade-marks, at least as a heel. Some people use rest holds. Me, I give my opponent a big power move and then run through a series of arrogant muscle poses for the crowd. This gave Violet time to roll around in her own vomit for awhile, and for the crowd to boo and otherwise hurl insults at me.

Actually the Dartmouth crowd was pretty good-natured about the whole thing and didn't get terribly personal. They just reacted to me as if I were an arrogant bitch who didn't even have the decency to wear a sexy outfit. I wore a pair of old camouflage pants, black wrestling boots, and a black spandex leotard. My theory was that as a villain I didn't want to give the crowd anything they could like about me, including how I dressed. Besides, I was still over 180 pounds at the time and while I could have put together an outfit that would have been flattering, it was easier just to go the Salvation Army route.

After a while, Flame grabbed my ankle. These days I listen to the crowd and use that as my barometer for when I think the babyface should start beating me up. But at this point I

163

pretty much left it up to Violet to attack me whenever she felt ready. She and I had a strange in-ring relationship for the first six months or so of my professional career. Usually the veteran and more experienced wrestler is the heel and directs the match, while the inexperienced wrestler is the babyface and for the most part follows the heel's lead. This isn't always the case, especially if you have a well-known veteran who has made her career as a babyface going up against a less experienced heel. But Violet was a five-year veteran, who had been both a heel and a baby, and the only thing I had done, both in training and in front of crowds, was heel. Plus I outweighed her by 50 pounds and had about four inches on Violet.

I wasn't told to go in that direction at wrestling school. One of the things that I tried to do right from the start, as I mentioned, was act like I was in front of a crowd in training. I might not be able to do the moves very well yet, but I still yelled, sold, registered, and in general acted like I was in Madison Square Garden and not working out in a wrestling school in downtown Malden, Massachusetts, in front of three wrestler's wives and two guys who were thinking about joining. And in doing this I found that my natural tendency was as a villain.

I think that a lot of this has to do with the fact that I find it easier to show my personality in ways that people enjoy more coming from a heel. Plus, as women go, I'm fairly muscular for a non-bodybuilder. I am also blessed with being a bit larger and more rugged-looking than most women, which are traits that serve a wrestler well as a villain. Think

The thing I like most about Violet is that she is fun to beat up

D.J. VON WYC

about it. The babyface is usually the underdog, either because she is smaller or because the heel cheats (or both).

Violet and I didn't really have a relationship where she called the matches and I followed her lead. At this point we hadn't actually had a full match yet. We were basically just running spots that we had practiced in class, so we were able to pretty much memorize our little routine in advance and just talk it over a little before our matches. This would all change fairly soon, but back to the match.

Flame grabbed my ankle and dumped me on my back. Walter shows all of his students ways to put someone on their back for real, but Violet and I were putting on a show so I went down as soon as she exerted the slightest amount of pressure on my leg. Then she went through her routine of doing mean things to my leg to see if she could break it. I forget what Violet did exactly, but it probably involved kicks to the hamstring and elbow drops to the inside of my thigh.

I made a fight of it, and then we worked our spot to where I was up against the ropes. So right on cue, Violet gave me a couple of boots and then a hard right hand, which I sold by sailing out of the ring backwards between the ropes and bouncing off the floor. She celebrated up in the ring while I sold down on the floor below. Her celebration was the baby-face equivalent of my posing routine earlier. When she thought the time was right, Violet came out onto the ring apron. I turned to face her and she jumped at me with the idea of splattering my brains all over Led Auditorium.

But instead I caught her in a bear hug. I had thought up

this little spot in wrestling school because Violet had broken her ankle some time ago and didn't want to jump off the apron and put pressure on it by landing on the floor.

"How about I just catch you?" I said one day in practice.

"Well, OK."

She was a little dubious at first, but we tried it a few times and it worked out just fine at the school and even better at the show. So I shook her around a bit and spun around so the crowd could see our faces. I turned around again, ran forward a few steps and drove Violet's back into the side of the ring. Then I gave her a couple of chops. Meanwhile, the referee had counted us both up to six. Before the match I told him that if Violet and I went out of the ring, not to count us out and if necessary come out after us. Apparently he had forgotten, so I looked up and gave him a significant look. It went right over the zebra's head.

"You aren't going to count us out, you idiot? Those four guys in there will kill you if I don't first!" I snarled up at the official. I was trying to remind him about what I said before the match but do it in a way that was entertaining for the fans.

Finally a light went on and the referee jumped out of the ring and started arguing with me. I bounced Flame's head off the apron a couple of times, rolled her back in the ring and then argued with the official a bit before climbing back in myself.

It was almost time to go home, so I softened Violet up with a few more kicks. Then I scraped her off the mat, put her in a full nelson and dragged her over to our corner. One of my guys had come out with a trash can lid, so we thought that would be a good way to transition into the finish of our match and get everyone involved at the end.

"Do it! Do it!" I screamed at Rotten. He was holding up the lid and looking around at the crowd. The people were starting to get noisy. I had just finished kicking Violet's ass and despite the fact that I was still very green, we had all gotten the situation where we wanted it. The people were feeling sorry for Violet already, and this huge guy menacing her with a big hunk of aluminum put us over the top. They definitely wanted to see her get away somehow and for the bad guys to get their just desserts.

That was when Freight Train came barreling out of his corner and started putting the forearms to Rotten. I let go of Flame and she got back on top of me, kicking and punching me into one of the corners while the guys worked into a free-for-all. Violet and I soon ended up brawling outside the ring, which with four guys in there seemed the safest bet. Meanwhile Freight Train climbed to the top rope. I was kind of curious what he was going to do. One thing about having six people fighting at once is that it is kind of hard to really plan anything out and even harder to have things go as planned. I hadn't done that many matches at that point, but I had seen guys do six-man tags at the school and even without a crowd watching they tend to turn a bit chaotic toward the end.

"Choo! Choo!" Freight Train yelled from the top as he pumped his arm like a train conductor hitting the air breaks. The crowds enjoy it when he does that. Especially the kids.

168

Slamming Violet on a mat that was baking from
a hundred degree heat. Ouch!

D.J. VON WYC

Then he leapt off the top and splattered Apocalypse all over the canvas. Violet and I brawled around to the other side of the ring, trying to work our way to the locker room.

Freight Train broke things up between me and Violet, allowing her to get back to the locker room. Shane was still attacking one of my guys so I jumped up to the ring to help him. Shane apparently wanted to hit a People's Elbow because

169

as I moved to intercept him he said, "No, please don't!" I didn't really know what to do so I made believe that my leg was still hurt from where Violet had beat on it during our match. This was probably a bit lame considering that I had just finished brawling with her a few seconds ago, but I didn't really know what else to do. The crowd didn't really seem to notice with everything that was going on though, so I just left my poor battered teammate to his fate and stomped back to the locker room.

All in all I was pleased with the match. I cringe when I think about these matches now, but it is very important to judge oneself by a contextual yardstick rather than by some unattainable or at least unrealistic standard. I had only been training a few months and hadn't really had much work in front of live crowds up to this point. Sure, I was inexperienced but Violet and I were able to run through everything we talked about correctly and reasonably smoothly. The thing that pleased me the most, looking back on the match, was that I had the presence of mind at the end to get Violet and I out of the ring away from the other four guys because it was safer. Afterwards, a couple of the veterans helped me by explaining what I could have done better, but they also said that I had a certain "ring sense" that was remarkable for someone who had only trained for a few months. And I'd made 25 dollars to boot.

One of the harsh realities about professional wrestling is that there isn't a lot of money for performers like me who have never been in a major federation. In fact, most of the guys I know make about 20 or 25 bucks to wrestle on a show. A lot of wrestling organizations don't pay most of their guys any-thing at all. There are so many young men who want to get in that ring and practice their craft in front of 50 or 100 people, that if one were to complain the promoter could just say, "Hey, if you don't like it there are 10 guys who want your spot."

It is a little different for a woman wrestler because there aren't 10 women waiting to take my spot. Heck, I don't think there are even 10 women in Massachusetts who could qual-ify as skilled wrestlers. So I can generally ask for more than 25 bucks to wrestle, but not much more. If I were to com-plain my spot wouldn't be taken; the promoter would just eliminate my spot altogether. So like just about every other independent wrestler out there I can't support myself through professional wrestling. I perform out of sheer love of the activity and a desire to practice and improve my craft. In a way we are like actresses who are putting our hearts and bodies on the line every weekend in little shows, each of us with dreams of the big time.

During my first year I was fortunate to have a husband who was willing to support me while I trained and concen-trated on wrestling. I made a lot of progress in my first year in terms of improving my performance in the ring and get-ting my name out there because I was free to concentrate on wrestling as a full-time job. A common misconception I often hear is that professional wrestlers are muscle-bound oafs. In fact most of them are pretty much like everyone else. Wrestlers generally hold the same sorts of jobs as everyone else. I've wrestled bartenders, nurses, realtors, a nutritionist, a firefighter, a doctor, an art dealer, and guys who say, "Would you like fries with that?" for a living. And believe it or not I've feuded with wrestlers who are still in high school.

The economics of wrestling dictate that most of us wrestle mainly in shows we can drive to in one day. Most wrestlers simply can't afford to drive for three days for basically nothing. Sometimes I'll carpool for a long drive with one of my "dread rivals," but for the most part I stick to shows in New England. I am able to command higher prices in New York because they have very strict licensing requirements, and a good female wrestler with a license is rarer than velociraptor teeth.

Very few federations will pay an undercard wrestler's travel expenses, which we call "trans." But some will contribute a little money for trans, and many feds that want to bring in quality talent will provide hotel rooms for their wrestlers. But by and large most wrestling companies do things on a shoestring and the wrestlers who work for them do likewise. For most of us, we keep our day jobs while we perform in armories, high schools, and bars all over North America while dreaming of that elusive limelight.

CHAPTER THIRTEEN

NOT THE LOCAL CABLE ACCESS

STORMDATE: April 9, 1999.

I was still riding high from my victory the week before. Yes, my side "lost" but no one got hurt, I had a good match relative to my skill at the time, the veterans had thought enough of me to give me advice *and* I was wrestling twice on two consecutive weekends. What more could a wrestling student like myself have asked for? (Besides a shot at the WWF title of course.)

This time I was wrestling at the Girls & Boys Club in Concord, New Hampshire, and was scheduled for an eight-man tag with some of the same participants as before. I was teamed up with Don Rotten and the guy named Cleon who got squashed a couple of months before, as well as the veteran King Kahula. My female counterpart was Violet Flame once again. She was teamed up with a tall blonde kid named Beau Douglas, Freight Train, and Tom O'Sullivan.

I came out first, leading my motley band of wrestlers to the beat of some Led Zeppelin song that at the time I thought was pretty cool. I climbed into the ring, walked over to one of the corners, and jumped onto the second rope. From there I hit my double biceps shot and sneered out at the crowd. This was fast becoming my usual act.

"Look at me! Look at this! I'm Amanda Storm! I'm the stone groove of the wrestling world!" I screamed. They of course responded with what were becoming the usual boo's.

Then I jumped up in the air and landed on the mat so that I made a lot of noise, then swaggered over to another corner and repeated the process to more raspberries. I didn't want to leave anyone out. These people came to be entertained and I wanted to do my best to make that happen and "Make the people notice me," as Walter Kowalski had exhorted me time and again.

Cleon was sitting on the top rope and told me to come over to him while the babyfaces made their entrance. So while our opponent's music played I got a nice neck massage courtesy of Cleon. A really nice guy. As Violet and the others were walking around the ring, I walked over and leaned out between the ropes. I had done this in Dartmouth and the fans seemed to enjoy it, so I thought that I'd try my little rant again.

"You're going down, honey!" I yelled. "I'm gonna destroy you! You're mine, baby!"

"You're the one going down," she replied. From there I just kept following Flame around from inside the ring berating her while she slapped hands with the fans. Once the babyfaces hit the ring we all bailed out and taunted the crowd in a more up close and personal kind of way.

Before the show several girls had come into the women's locker room. Usually the fans are kept out of the changing room but this was the only women's restroom in the club, so what could you do? Violet and I didn't even try to make believe we were enemies. Sure these kids were young but they weren't stupid. So instead we just hung out with them, chatted, and had a good time. The girls seemed excited to see actual women wrestlers. They apparently hadn't considered that there would actually be wrestlers *they* had something in common with. I firmly believe that skilled women wrestling in women's matches and especially bigger gals wrestling similarly sized men is a potential gold mine waiting to be tapped. If I am ever a promoter or a booker, I will do my best to schedule more of these types of matches.

I really liked one of the girls, whose name was Ashley. She was very sweet and I was quite charmed by how nice she seemed. Most kids I've met are cool but they have a certain selfishness about them that they only learn to mask when they get older. But Ashley struck me as having a natural openness and giving nature that you just don't often see in children. As she was leaving, Ashley said something about how she wished that she were special. I guess her feelings had been hurt earlier in the day by some boy who had said some mean things to her.

"You *are* special, Ashley," I said. Meanwhile the promoter came in with the guys and told us to put our match together with me taking the pin from Violet. I pulled Ashley to the side and continued because I couldn't let this sweet child out of my grasp without saying my piece. "Don't let anyone tell you that you aren't special. You *are* special because you are the only Ashley in the world. If people say mean things about you, then feel sorry for them because if they were truly happy they wouldn't spend their time hurting other people. But most importantly, strive to be your best and don't let other people drag you down."

I gave her a necklace that I wore to the event and she left, and I talked over the match with the guys. Mostly I listened while Kahula and the other veterans laid out the groundwork for the match, though Violet and I did contribute our ideas. The promoter stuck his head through the door again about five minutes later.

"Uh, Amanda is getting the pin on Violet," he said. Jim Gerard, who was still getting material for his magazine article, had arrived at the show. The promoter figured that since a freelancer for a major magazine had come to see Amanda Storm, he might as well put the girl over.

We started out the match with Freight Train getting the best of first Rotten and then Cleon. Once they had established that Freight Train could wrestle and got the fans to like him, it was time to piss off the fans by having Cleon and Don cut him off with some double team tactics. Then we got poor Freight Train on the ropes and with the referee properly distracted the four of us proceeded to pummel him completely senseless, to the intense displeasure of the audience.

It was this point in the match where, if this had been on television, the commentator would have been obligated to shout, "How can the referee allow this?!" The babyfaces piled into the ring to save F.T. and the whole affair quickly turned into an eight-wrestler free-for-all, with each of us fighting our assigned partner.

I gave Violet a quick boot and after we traded a few punches I slapped a quick headlock on her and worked it, all the while making sure neither of us got tangled up with the guys. Soon it was time for the ladies to do their thing once again. We did basically a lot of the same things as in

You'd think we'd get enough of this stuff in the ring
D.J. VON WYC

Dartmouth, but we expanded our act a bit and put a little more time in the ring. The flying clothesline, chops, and a nice simple bodyslam (where I hold the other person up for a few seconds and launch into an arrogant posing routine after dropping them) were becoming staples in my embryonic heel repertoire. Then it was Violet's turn to take over and do her stuff. This is how I described the rest of the match on my Web site:

> I felt a hand on my back and someone spinning me around, and who was it but that bitch, Violet Flame! She slugged me in the mouth and then started kicking me in the guts once I was up against the ropes. Then she shot me off but I reversed it and tried to take her head off with a roundhouse. Unfortunately, Flame is about three feet tall so she was able to duck and come back with an elbow of her own. Then she tried to pin me! I couldn't believe it. How dare she?! The audacity! The impudence! The arrogance!
>
> Well, unlike that old king in *Conan* I did not salute her. Instead I raked her eyes. Or at least I tried to. But she was kind of sweaty so I couldn't get a good grip on her head, so Flame started giving *me* the boot to the guts. And before you know it I was sailing out of the ring on my way to visit Mr. Concrete Floor. I don't know if you get tired of looking at pictures of me flying out of wrestling rings the hard way, but I certainly do and this was definitely no exception.

King Kahula helped me back into the ring and I thought it was time to break things up a bit by tagging out. Violet responded by immediately tagging out as well. Before the match the announcer made sure the fans knew about a stipulation that the guys couldn't wrestle the girls. Now, I've always considered rules to be something more akin to guidelines, and I wanted to show the fans that a woman could fight a man fairly and still beat the snot out of him. At least this woman could. So I tagged in when Beau was putting the heat to one of our guys. The only problem was, Douglas didn't want to fight me. I tried slapping him across the face. No luck. All he did was yammer at the referee, who, being a man, took my opponent's side. So I pressed the issue by planting my boot in Beau's gut and beating the tar out of him in the corner.

I had something to prove so I stepped back and let Beau out of the corner. Unfortunately what I succeeded in doing was making my opponent angry. He came charging out at me like some huge, 260-pound bull and picked me up for a slam. I knew this was going to tickle, so I kicked my legs in an effort to throw him off balance. It didn't work, so right when I was winding up to punch him in the crotch, Beau gently set me down and just turned to walk away. So far everything had proceeded according to plan.

I spun Douglas around and hoisted him up for a slam instead, with screams from the crowd of "Oh my God!" It wasn't easy either, because I held Beau up for a few seconds before I launched him at the mat. Judging by the screams and cheers of the fans, I think I made my point in aces and spades!

Mission accomplished, I tagged out and gave some of the boys a chance to strut their stuff again.

I was extremely pleased with how the spot with Beau went. This was the first time I had really done anything resembling a wrestling move in a show with anyone other

Another bleach blonde bites the dust!
D.J. VON WYC

NOT THE LOCAL CABLE ACCESS

than Violet, and not only did it go off as planned, we got a nice pop from the crowd to boot.

As the match wore on, Cleon distracted the referee while King Kahula and I beat down Violet. Then I scraped her up off the mat with the idea that one of my guys would clomp her on the head with a street sign. (I guess I didn't learn my lesson from Dartmouth the week before.) This time we worked the ending a little differently (and to be honest, I wish we had brought the trash can lid again). Instead of having Freight Train save the day, Flame ducked and my team-mate hit me in the head instead.

"Make sure you hit her on top of the head with the sign," Kahula had said before the match. "You can make good contact and not hurt Amanda as long as you hit her on top of the head."

Well, my guy didn't want to hurt me, which I appreciate immensely, but he gave me a glancing blow that caught me near the temple with the edge of the sign. It hurt like hell and didn't look or sound nearly as good as a solid, flat blow on the top of my skull. That just goes to show, when you are afraid of a move — either for yourself or someone else — the chances of it looking ugly increase dramatically. I didn't take it too hard, though. I didn't get busted open, it didn't leave a nasty scar later, and the crowd seemed to like the whole scenario just fine. Besides, my "assailant's" heart was in the right place and you can't find fault with that. Naturally Violet went for the pin. This is probably how the match would have ended if Jim Gerard hadn't been in attendance. So, thanks go out to

Jim for being instrumental in Amanda Storm getting her first pinfall in a professional wrestling show. I enjoyed it, which was good because this was the first and the last for quite some time to come.

While the referee was distracted yet again, King Kahula dragged Violet to her feet and gave her a quick DDT. He then rolled my carcass over on top of the prone Violet, allowing me to get the pin in true heel fashion. The referee and Kahula both raised my hands in victory, but the celebration was short lived because the match ended in a big melee, with Beau tossing me into the corner and then out of the ring. I took what I thought was a nice bump almost into the first row, though I was careful not to hurt any of the fans. I have a screenshot from a video my husband shot of the match and all you can see are my feet sticking up in the air. I know it looked like a good bump because our manager, Rotten Robbie, helped me up and whispered, "Are you OK?"

I staggered to my feet and then went after the street sign guy (I won't say who he is here) and gave him a kick in the small of the back and then planted him face-first into the wall. The fans loved it as I bounced my former partner off the architecture and dragged him into the women's dressing room where we all started laughing. It was a good match, the fans were entertained, and no one got overly hurt.

During intermission I got to sign autographs and I had a blast meeting the fans. I might be a "natural heel" but I am definitely a babyface when it comes to the people who pay to see the show. I absolutely love talking to the kids and reminiscing with the older people about Killer Kowalski and some of the stars from decades gone by. But the part I like best is when a child goes away from talking to Amanda Storm happy and his or her parent looks me in the eye and silently says, "Thank you." That to me is worth all of the sweat and pain I put up with in my effort to put on a good performance and constantly improve.

The Concord tag went well, but a lot happened outside the ring that night as well. I went out and actually managed to sell a few pictures during intermission and signed a ton of autographs, which made me happy. I found it especially gratifying that Violet and I were both surrounded by girls, who were enthusiastic about seeing women wrestlers in action. Most of what goes on at independent wrestling shows isn't really targeted at girls. The boys have plenty of wrestlers to identify with and cheer or boo. The girls, on the other hand, usually have a couple of valets who don't really do all that much or — worse yet — are basically eye candy. So it isn't surprising that young women often feel a little left out, and I'm glad when I can do my part to change that situation a little bit.

King Kong Bundy was up in the ring "doing polaroids" which basically meant that fans were lining up to have their picture taken with Chris for five dollars a pop. I wanted to have my photo taken with him but I didn't want to seem like a mark. Of course, the biggest marks in wrestling are the wrestlers themselves. Think about it. Fans generally pay a few bucks and drive across town to sit and be entertained for a couple of hours. Wrestlers, on the other hand, devote tremendous amounts of time and money to training. They risk serious injury for little or no pay and often drive insane distances just to pretend they are beating each other up. Then many of them stand around the back and talk about this person being a mark and that person being a mark. Let's face it, we're all marks, boys. That's part of what lends pro wrestling its charm.

If I were a fan I would enjoy knowing that the performers were motivated mainly by the sheer love of their calling. This is what makes "amateur" athletics more fun to watch than "professional" sports where the participants are paid insane amounts of money and talk about hitting a ball with a stick being a "business." I understand that when you do something for a living you have to approach it as a business. But as a fan, isn't it a lot more fun to root for players whom you know are motivated by their love of the game and not their love of a paycheck? So while we may call it professional wrestling, in reality what we do makes sports fun to watch. But back to Chris.

Of course I couldn't just have my picture taken. I had to make a big show of it, and I think Chris found me a little amusing. I waited until most of the fans were done and then I came out to ringside. "Oh my God!" I screamed. "It's King Kong Bundy! Can I have my picture taken with you, Mr. Bundy?" I was waving a five-dollar bill like a john at a strip show who is trying to entice his favorite dancer to let him cop a feel in return for a little money.

"Put that away, Storm!" Chris said as he laughed and waved me up into the ring. So I got my Polaroid with Chris, and it went up on the Web site the very next day, where it still

*Good times with
King Kong "Call me
Chris" Bundy in
New Hampshire*
D.J. VON WYC

proudly lives in my gallery. I don't know how important this event was for my career but it sure was a lot of fun.

I went back to the women's locker room with my trophy and deposited the picture in my bag. Then I went and hung out near some pool tables in the front lobby. There were a few fans milling about as well as some wrestlers. My performance for the evening was over, but wrestling was still new enough to me that I wanted to stay and enjoy the rest of the show. I was hoping someone would ask me for my autograph and I could casually sign their paper like it was no big deal, all the while secretly marking out for myself.

While I was standing around I noticed that there were an awful lot of guys floating about with some very expensive video equipment. One of them set his camera down on the pool table near me and started leafing through some papers.

My goal was to find out who they were and get in on whatever publicity they were offering. But how to accomplish this? If I just asked the fellow who he was with, then he would probably tell me and go back to his paperwork and not even want to know anything about this raven-haired beauty in a tank top standing next to him.

I could see that a couple of girls were about to walk up and ask for my autograph. They had that slightly nervous, hopeful look on their faces that one sees on the very young in such situations. So I walked over to the other side of the pool table as they approached so the camera guy couldn't help but see the exchange. I noticed out of the corner of my eye that he was starting to notice me as I answered one of the girl's questions about what it was like being a wrestler. Excellent. She couldn't have helped me more if she had been my own daughter that I had coached into playing the role.

Once the girls left I walked up to him.

"Hi."

"Hi," he replied.

"You aren't the local cable access, are you?" I said, grinning impishly. At least I tried to look impish. He laughed and asked me my name and I told him.

"We're from MTV," he told me, "and we're filming a documentary on independent wrestling. Would you mind if we shot a little footage of you?"

"That would be fine. I'd like that," I said, trying not to immediately launch into an Amanda Storm dance of joy.

So the camera guy stuck his lens in my face and told me

186

to "say something." I don't remember what I said exactly, though I remember doing a lot of flexing, ranting, and opening my mouth for the camera and asking if "he wanted to see my fillings." He asked me a lot of other questions too, and I did my best to come up with witty, interesting answers to "make the people notice me." It seemed to work.

The interviewer asked me about my "character" and I wanted to say something different than what other wrestlers were probably saying. So I did something that you don't see much anymore in wrestling (and certainly not with this book) and I indulged in a little kayfabe.

"Character? That would imply that wrestling isn't real. I don't have a character. I'm Amanda Storm. I'm Amanda Storm in real life and what you see is what you get."

When he asked me about "props" I said, "We prefer to call them 'weapons'" and so forth.

There was some truth in what I was saying. Unlike some wrestlers, I didn't really set out to create an artificial persona for the ring. Heck, except for my boots my costumes are basically just workout gear or bathing suits. And how I act is more Amanda the person cutting loose and just acting crazy and uninhibited, whether as a face or heel, than it is me portraying some character. One of the beautiful things about wrestling is that I have license to act absolutely crazy and I love it!

The documentary, though I didn't know it at the time, was True Life: I Am a Pro Wrestler. The show has run dozens of times on MTV over the past year and is probably responsible for turning more people on to Amanda Storm than any other piece of publicity to date. My plan was to try and be interesting, but to say things that would sound and look good in small doses. I knew that the documentary wasn't about Amanda Storm, so if I was going to be a part of it then I had to give them a product that would look good pared down into three- to five-second sound bites. The guy then had me sign a release and write down some contact information and said they would be in touch.

I noticed in all of this that Tony Atlas was sitting by himself off in a corner looking, well, pissed off. I didn't really know the man terribly well so I didn't think it wise to ask him what was going on. I was very curious though, because the show seemed to be going well and MTV was covering it. What was there to be upset about? I thought. I would learn in due course.

Meanwhile, the MTV folks seemed fairly interested in getting footage so I talked a couple more of the cameramen, who were just sitting around, into taping a little skit that I devised. I figured that the more footage of Amanda Storm I could convince them to take, the better the chances of the editor and producer finding something they could use in the show.

So I hunted down Violet Flame and sort of pressed her into service. Then I cut a promo talking about how I beat Violet and all of her wimpy friends in our match, and how I could beat her again easily and so on. I don't remember what I said exactly because I ad libbed most of it. A wrestler has to be able to launch into something interesting on the spur of the moment, and I noticed this from the very beginning. I only have a few seconds to capture the attention of the fans in a match or a reporter in the back, and that first impression can make the difference between my getting noticed or having half the crowd get up and leave.

It amazes me how many very skilled wrestlers are terrified of the microphone and the camera. I think this holds a lot of very good wrestlers back, because they think that professional wrestling is about the moves you do in the ring. I don't claim to have all the answers, but in my experience professional wrestling is about making people care about your character and then giving them a match that is entertaining. I have seen matches where the wrestlers basically proved to me that it was indeed possible to break the laws of physics, but no one noticed because they were all getting popcorn. And then I've seen matches where the audience was coming unglued over a headlock.

Anyway, right in the middle of my promo, Violet stomped in and "cold cocked" me and then smashed my face into a steel table. I fell to the floor and from there we started brawling and the camera faded away. Unfortunately that footage apparently ended up on the cutting room floor because it wasn't in the show, but it was good practice just the same. I got to cut a promo in front of two MTV cameras and even do a little fight scene. All the while Tony Atlas just sat there watching with his hands folded and a dejected look on his face. I was going to try and involve him by shouting something at him during my promo but I could tell that he wanted to be left alone so I gave him his space. His look was a harbinger of things to come very shortly, but not that day. That day was a good one, at least for Amanda Storm.

CHAPTER FOURTEEN

"NO SHOW TONITE!"

STORMDATE: April 10, 1999.

I went home to Maine basically in triumph. Not only did the Concord show go well and I got a shot at appearing on MTV, but there was another show the next night right up the road from my house, and then yet another one in Springfield, Massachusetts. Three shows in three days. It couldn't get much better than that.

I showed up at the Lewiston multi-purpose center ready to rumble. A crew was setting up the ring, and a few of the wrestlers were already there, as well as the usual entourage of girlfriends, people trying to get into wrestling, and so on. Something didn't seem quite right, though. Where was James St. Jean and the other people who were in charge of setting up and running the show?

Tony Atlas was helping to set up chairs and he had a

worried look on his face that I didn't like one bit. I quickly found out that whether or not there would be a show at all had become questionable. I didn't know what to do, so I helped set up some chairs and told Tony that if there was anything I could do to let me know.

Rumors were starting to go around that something was wrong, and indeed the ring crew stopped working on setting up the ring. When some of the wrestlers, who were apparently booked for the show, started showing up from Massachusetts, the shit *really* started to hit the fan. Apparently no one had told them that there was no show, and at least one had driven from as far away as New Jersey — a nine-hour drive — expecting to wrestle. (No one had told me either, but I only lived a couple of towns over.)

It was a shame, because local television had shown up and was interviewing some of the wrestlers, and MTV was there again. Plus, fans were starting to line up outside the door and it was promising to be a good show. The crumpled blue sign someone had hastily taped on the door which now read "Show Canceled" wasn't exactly inspiring anyone with confidence, either.

The problem was that James St. Jean, the promoter of record for the event, was the only person who had a license to actually run the show. I didn't know much about the process at the time, but according to the Athletic Commission in Maine you need a promoter's license for each town to run a show. So you can have a license that allows you to put on a wrestling event in Lewiston, Maine, but that doesn't mean you can host

"Here's a kiss for you, tough boy"
D.J. VON WYC

a show anywhere else without a separate license. And apparently James was the only person who had a promoter's license for *anywhere* in Maine. No one in the multi-purpose center at the time had one.

Mainly I stayed out of the way because there wasn't much I could do, but my husband and I told Tony that we would help if we could. I gave Tony our cell phone so he could call around and see if he could find anyone on short notice with a license. He called the boxer, Joey Gamache, who apparently had let his license expire, and a few other people but no dice. Then the commissioner showed up and that was when he, Tony, and a few other people went behind closed doors to have a discussion. I wasn't in the room but the long and short of it was no one had a promoter's license so there couldn't be a show and there was no way that Tony was going to obtain

192

a license on the day of the show.

While all of this was going on, I went into "how can Amanda salvage something positive out of this" mode. I was standing near the half-set-up ring watching the two guys who were busy setting it up earlier horsing around trying to give each other powerbombs but only succeeding in dropping each other on their heads.

"Mind if I try something?" I asked one of them.

"No, that'd be cool. Come on up," the smaller of the two said. I don't remember his name or really what he looked like but he was wearing a blue shirt. This was when the local television station was interviewing some wrestlers.

"I'm Amanda and I was supposed to wrestle here tonight."

"Really? You're a wrestler?" the guy in the blue shirt asked.

"Yipper dog."

"Huh?"

"Yes, I'm a wrestler. I see you've had a little training. Mind if we do a couple of spots?"

So I put him through a short sequence of moves where I basically threw him around, acted like I was in front of 500 people, made a lot of noise, and bodyslammed the poor guy to the mat. Fortunately most of the ring was already set up. It was just the ropes that hadn't been attached and some cosmetic stuff still needed to be taken care of, like the skirting.

I had one eye on the reporter interviewing Robbie Ellis, and he walked over to the ring after we were finished.

"Hi, I'm Rob Caldwell."

"Hello. Amanda Storm. I was supposed to wrestle tonight," I said as we shook hands.

"Can you do some of that stuff again while we have the camera on you?" he asked.

He didn't have to exactly twist anyone's arm to get us jumping around again. I think I yelled something about ruling the world or asking if he wanted to see my fillings, but I don't remember exactly. It was all pretty much spur of the moment. But it had the desired effect. Rob asked me a few questions and told me that he was supposed to do a piece on the show. Rob said that he was very interested in talking with me more and perhaps in doing a story. He wasn't able to discuss any specifics at that moment because he already had an assignment. So we exchanged business cards, I thanked the ring crew guy, and we went our separate ways.

More importantly, the guys from MTV were interested in me again. They were there to film Tony wrestling, which obviously wasn't going to happen. So instead they documented what had happened, which was the show in Lewiston being canceled and the aftermath which followed. Plus, the MTV boys were going to come over to your humble narrator's house and interview her in the next day or so; they had some free time on their hands. Actually, besides the show in Lewiston, there was supposed to be yet another show in Springfield, Massachusetts, the day after the Lewiston show, which was also canceled.

So things were looking very good for Amanda, and part

of me was on Cloud Nine. I felt like I had salvaged some gold from a sinking ship, but another part of me felt terrible. A lot of people were hurt and angry about the shows being canceled. The parents were upset because they wanted to see wrestling, and more importantly they were angry because their kids were really looking forward to the show. Some of the children were even crying. Now I have this maternal side that I don't like to admit to, but I have to say that there is something inside Amanda Storm that just makes her fall to pieces when she sees a little girl bawling her eyes out. I had a few of my "Share the Evil" T-shirts in my bag that I gave away, as well as some pictures, to try and make some of them feel better. I doubt that most of them knew who I was, but giving that stuff to the kids made me feel good at least.

I have avoided saying too much publicly about the whole conflagration between Tony and James. What you are reading here is the most I have talked about this situation in a public forum. I have heard a lot of stories about "Wrestler X stole money," and "Wrestler Y only paid his friends," but I had no way of really knowing what went on beyond my own experience, which was a mixed bag. There are usually two sides to every story, and I have since learned that the only thing that makes this misunderstanding special was the fact that MTV made a show about it. This sort of foolishness goes on every weekend in independent wrestling. These are just the sort of antics we wrestlers think of when we say that the "hardest part about wrestling is the politics and games." I could see that the best course of action for a small fish like Amanda

Storm was to just keep going to wrestling school and not get involved. At least not yet.

Speaking of politics, no one from the EWA called to let me know that the shows were canceled, but I did find this e-mail from St. Jean waiting for me when I got home from the multi-purpose center:

Storm,
There is NO show tonite or in Springfield!!!

Apparently James and Tony had had some problems involving money. I wasn't privy to their dealings and my knowledge of the whole sorry argument comes from hearing both sides as well as the swirl of rumors that surrounded the brouhaha for months afterwards. James's camp advocated that Tony Atlas was a crook and a cheat. Tony's camp argued that James was a crook and a cheat, as well as an "asshole" for calling Tony a "boy" on the MTV special and saying that "wrestlers are used to not getting paid."

My feeling on the matter, from what I saw and not what I heard, was that the truth was somewhere in the middle. Tony and James didn't really have any sort of system or controls in place for efficiently handling the money or delegating responsibility. Finally, once their promotion grew past a certain level, problems came up that neither man could solve, at least not as a team. So James, apparently perceiving that he was losing money with Tony, cut bait and canceled the next two shows. What Mr. St. Jean does with his money and whether he chooses to run a wrestling show is his business, but in my opinion, he really should have called up the wrestlers and showed up in person to let the fans know. I am not saying that Tony Atlas is blameless for what happened. I know Tony pretty well and he is the last person to say that he is perfect. But the fact remains that he showed up and did his best to put on a wrestling show. And he and I were the ones who had to go out and apologize to the fans when there was no wrestling that night.

I didn't really know it at the time, but forces were moving that would radically alter the course of my attempts at a wrestling career. I was ready to quit wrestling for James right then and there, but Tony talked me out of it. He told me that what I needed most was time in the ring in front of crowds, and that was what I should focus on and not worry about anything else. He was right and I'm glad I took his advice. In the meantime there were three more shows for the Eastern Wrestling Alliance.

CHAPTER FIFTEEN

MALE CREDIBILITY

STORMDATE: April 24, 1999.

The show at the University of Machias was something of a turning point for me: it was the first time I was scheduled to wrestle a man in a show. Sure, most of my training was with the boys down at Walter's, but not counting a few spots in mixed tags, the only person I had ever wrestled in a live event was Violet. I had not even so much as talked to this guy before.

But Violet couldn't make the show because Machias was an insane distance from where she lived in Massachusetts. Machias is in extreme south-eastern Maine, often nicknamed "Down East." It was quite a drive for me too, even though I live in Maine. I took more than one wrong turn on a nameless dirt road and during the trip I saw two deer, almost hit a skunk, ran over a dead turkey, and had an unconfirmed Bigfoot sighting.

MALE CREDIBILITY

My opponent for the evening was one Jack "The Slayer" Crow. He was about my size, which was good, and not bad looking, which was very good. I say this because I wanted to stay with my cheating ways for this match. I had always played a heel and if we worked the match correctly the crowd might actually feel sorry for Jack and want to see him beat me. Now if Jack were some ugly guy then that probably wouldn't have worked as well. The Amanda Storm who is writing this now could and has had good matches as a heel against lots of big, ugly guys but there have been a lot of sessions down at Kowalski's and a lot of shows between the time I am typing this page and that day down in Machias.

We talked for about 10 minutes about wrestling and other stuff we liked to do, and in general got to know each other a little. Jack seemed a little dubious about the match, but he came across as a good sport and a genuinely nice guy. When it came down to brass tacks though, the fact of the matter was that both of us wanted to be in the ring and we both would have jobbed to the ring crew if that was what we had to do.

Eventually we made our way to the ring and began talking over what we were going to do in our match. This was when I got a chance to talk to Steve Ramsey. I had met Steve at my very first show back in January, but we didn't really talk at all. Apparently he had some hand in Jack's training and wanted to help us prepare for our match. At first I was pleased and grateful that Steve was willing to share the benefit of his experience with us.

"Who is going over?" he asked.

Dishing out a
little abuse to
poor Tony Atlas
D.J. VON WYC

"James hasn't told us yet," Jack said. I just nodded in agreement.

"Oh, well, no offense, Amanda. I know that you're a worker and all but you have to put over Jack. He has his male credibility to think about." Now I know that this story is going to get me in dutch with certain people when they read my book. That is the problem with writing a biography at the beginning of your career rather than at the end. I will still have to deal with many of the people I'm writing about once this thing hits the stores. But it wouldn't be much of a book if I weren't honest, so I'll damn the torpedoes and press on.

By the look on Jack's face, this seemed to be news to him. I couldn't believe it and wanted to tell Ramsey to screw off in the worst way, but I just nodded quietly and listened. One thing I have learned from wrestling school was to give veterans a certain amount of respect and deference, and to think before I open my mouth. Besides, at that point in time he wasn't the booker.

Steve just stood there and looked at me. Apparently he was waiting for an answer. "Um, well, I've only gone over once so far so if James asks me to job that's fine with me. Either way though, I don't care as long as we both have a good match."

Ramsey seemed to like this answer.

"I'll go find out what is going on," he said and left.

Rotten Robbie showed up while Jack and I were talking. Robbie was going to be my manager, which was good, because we could use him to help me cheat and establish right off the bat where things stood. The "male credibility" thing did give me an idea though. . . .

Jack came to the ring first and while I was making my entrance, he complained to high heaven about "having to fight a woman." Crow kept turning his back on me as he argued with the promoter, the referee, and some of the fans about the match. One of the things that Walter Kowalski told me was that you should never turn your back on your opponent in a wrestling match or let him turn his back on you, because that is the ultimate form of disrespect.

So I had Rotten Robbie hand me up a chair and while he

distracted the referee I clobbered Jack square in the back. One thing about my chair shots is that they hurt. I do them correctly of course, because I have respect for the people I wrestle, but my feeling is that if you are going to hit someone with a chair then lay it in and make some noise. These guys who half hit someone just don't get it in my book. They make themselves and their opponents look foolish. Plus, it devalues the shock value of using something like a chair. When you hit someone with a piece of furniture, they should most definitely writhe about in pain for awhile unless they are in ECW. And that is just what Jack did in a figurative sense.

At this point the crowd, who originally wanted to cheer the natural underdog — namely me — now started rooting for Crow. I ignored him and instead concentrated on yelling out at the crowd, picking out certain people to insult and arrogantly flexing my muscles. The time was right for Jack to get a little revenge.

Crow finally got up and spun me around, laying into me with punches, chops, kicks, clotheslines, and that sort of unpleasantness. One of my specialties seemed to be getting knocked out of the ring. I knew at least 10 different ways to launch myself out of or over a wrestling ring. Sure enough Crow tossed me through the ropes onto the floor. We had planned for him to come out after me still fired up and plant my face on the apron. But one of the security guys leaned over and asked me if I was all right. Apparently I had done a very convincing job of appearing to hit my head on the floor.

When Jack came out I could see that he wasn't sure what

to do. I think he picked up on the security guard's concern and thought I might be hurt. (Looking back on the match, it was awfully nice of him to care. A lot of wrestlers would have been so busy trying to get themselves over with the fans that they wouldn't have time to worry about if their opponent was hurt.) So he was helping me up and looking concerned, which actually got him over even better with the fans. This crazy girl hit him with a chair and then gloated about it. This made the fans mad and they were definitely with him as he got up and tossed her ass out of the ring. But then he started having second thoughts, and being a gentleman and all, he went out to help the poor girl up. Maybe this whole thing was a mistake and they could shake hands and leave as friends.

Nope. I took control of the match again and planted his face on the apron, because we were about two feet from the fans and I couldn't very well just say, "Oh, I'm fine, Jack, let's just keep going, old bean. Chip chip and God save the Queen!" No, that just wouldn't do at all. Strangely enough it all worked out. The crowd got mad again because not only was I treacherous but I was responding to chivalry with yet more backstabbing. I heard more than one person call me a bitch. I was loving it!

Jack and I went back and forth a little, but by the end of the match he was getting the better of me. It was time to finish the evil Amanda Storm off. So Crow climbed to the top, but I was a bit tougher than he thought, and slowly struggled to my feet. Unfortunately for me he kicked me in the face and jumped off the top rope, catching me with a sunset flip. It could have ended right there and we all could have gone home with poor Jack's male credibility safely intact. But I summoned up what little strength I had left for women everywhere and kicked out on two. It was time to end this thing. This is how I described it on my Web site:

> I jumped out of the ring, grabbed the offending bit of furniture that had started everything and threw it back into the ring. Crow snatched up the chair before the referee could intercept him. (Fool! You are blundering right into my trap!) I climbed back into the ring and backed up against the ropes, "begging" Jack not to lay into me. (Bwahahahaha!!!) But his blood was up and he'd have none of that. This next part is priceless. (God, I love it when a plan comes together.) I ducked as he swung the chair squarely at my head. Crow hit the ropes so hard that the chair bounced back and he plastered himself square in the chops. The idiot had knocked himself out cold! The referee could hardly disqualify me for my opponent knocking himself out, so he reluctantly put hand to canvas and beat out the Crow one, two, three. The sweetest song a girl can ever hear. Then the ref started arguing with me. I guess he didn't like the cut of my jib or something, so I laid him out too — the match being over and all — and applied the second count myself.

All in all I was pleased with the match. The only thing in

the match that truly bothered me was that we both got a little scare when I picked up Crow for a body slam and one of the boards almost gave. I actually staggered and almost lost my footing while I was holding the poor guy up. Thank goodness that I'm fairly strong and we were working together cooperatively because otherwise professional wrestling might have been minus one Jack Crow, which I would have had to live with for the rest of my life.

Don't we make a lovely couple?
CAMERABOY

That incident made me change how I come into the ring. Sure, I'm still the same crazy chick that screams, "I hate you all!" or that smiling girl in red, white, and blue or red and white (depending on if I'm a Canadian or an American) who passes out candy to the audience, but I also walk all around the ring and get a sense for how the boards feel. I grab the ropes and test how tight they are and I sneak a look at the turnbuckles while the referee is checking out my opponent's boots.

The only other bad thing about the match was the crowd — there wasn't much of one and I felt bad for the college. I talked to the woman who was in charge of organizing the event and apparently no one had told her that she was responsible for advertising the event until a week before the show. Quite reasonably, she started to wonder why she wasn't seeing any posters or hearing anything about wrestling coming to her school. So the EWA pretty much killed wrestling in that town.

CHAPTER SIXTEEN

"OBEY MY VOICE YOUNG DEMON"

STORMDATE: June 1999.

There were a couple of more shows for the EWA, but they were basically repeat performances of things I have already done and talked about. I was still going to wrestling school and getting a little more comfortable in front of crowds, though I still needed a lot more work. But there were forces that had been at play behind the scenes in the passing months after the mess with the cancelled shows back in April. There had been rumors flying around, wrestlers splintering into factions, semi-private meetings, and all sorts of political wrangling. None of it really concerned your narrator, because she just went on doing her thing, oblivious that Chaos was about to come crashing down upon her little wrestling world.

One fine, summer day everything was right with the world. I had been training hard and doing everything I could to shine in my matches. I was jobbing of course and concentrating on improving and trying to get comfortable in front of the fans. But I had a show coming up that I was looking forward to with great anticipation. Yes, Amanda Storm was about to win her third match and her first women's championship. I realize that as a performer, wrestling is first about entertaining the fans and not about winning the matches, which are obviously pre-determined. But there was a small part of me that was excited. I have to admit that every morning I would do my business in the bathroom and then take a deep breath and give my best Amanda Storm leer into the mirror. I would look first to my left and then to the right, then pause. I would bring my microphone (my toothbrush actually) up to my mouth with a snarl.

"So how does it feel, folks? You are witnessing a historic moment, a changing of the guard, the beginning of a dynasty. Yes, I am now officially what women's wrestling is all about and I think of this belt as a crown!"

I would wave around my towel and shake it a little for the imaginary fans to gaze upon as they expressed their displeasure.

"I am no longer just Amanda Storm. I am now the Women's Champion, and you must call me Queen Amanda! That's right, bow down before me, for I am your Ruler! No, Queen Amanda is all that and more. She is your Rassling God!"

Then I would launch into a fit of my ridiculous muscle poses that experience had taught me make the fans love to hate me. All in the privacy of my own bathroom with my hopes, my imagination, and that part of me that was still a little girl who dreamed of someday being a wrestler.

Reality struck later that day. One of my wrestling mentors called me aside and gently told me that he didn't want me to work for James St. Jean anymore. That hurt. Actually it more than hurt. Despite the bad things that went along with working for James, his shows were the only ones I was doing up to this point. I felt like a rug had been pulled out from under me and my wrestling career was over. God, I tried to keep a straight face but I almost started crying right then and there. All of the anticipation, the hard work, the bruises, and the dieting and now I felt like I had nothing left. Like I said before, I was overreacting but at the time it felt like the Hammer of Thor.

So I crept off to the 7–11, pounded down a pint of Ben & Jerry's Chocolate Chip Cookie Dough ice cream, had a good cry, and drove home ready to quit wrestling entirely. I was sick of the politics, the lying, and the games. When I got home I engaged in that last refuge of the depressed and put my feelings down on paper. I know I'm depressed when my thoughts turn to William Blake. (Yes, it was that bad):

> The creature throws out moist, invisible tentacles
> that wrap themselves around me
> and suck at my flesh with vampiric urgency.
> My screams dissolve into exhausted, impotent cries
> as the worm envelopes me in its slimy, vibrating web.
> The cocoon (or is it an egg?) begins to shiver.
> Gently at first.

209

BLAKWIDOW

Its baneful energy increases . . .
feeding upon itself like an intelligent cancer . . .
a diseased crescendo climaxing with a fervid quaking . . .
the egg bloats and hemorrhagic cracks bloom on its surface,
like infernal rosebuds opening to a warm, spring rain in Hell.
They melt like so much sentient wax.
The mucous shell splits
revealing a leucotic, mummified butterfly.
The insect lifts itself into the air by willpower alone;
its shriveled, palsied wings are riddled with holes.

I was drifting in and out of consciousness,
(and all the while this is a dream — talk about
infinite regress!)
when I perceived a sound, a voice,
pronouncing words with a rasping monotone lisp,
structuring sentences into an infected iambic pentameter:
"Obey my voice young Demon I am God
from Eternity to Eternity."
"Yes."
"Mark well my words: they are of your ever-
lasting salvation or your damnation."
I reeled as my brain shivered and expanded,
then contracted,
like a dying star,
forming a dead, chitinous lump of echopractic tar.

My mentor wasn't terribly impressed that many of his wrestlers drove over a hundred miles — in some cases over 200 or even 300 — for nothing and that St. Jean didn't even give them the courtesy of a phone call. And he wasn't too pleased that many of these wrestlers were his students, yours truly included, though I only lived over in the next town from where the canceled shows were supposed to take place.

In retrospect, once I calmed down I realized that my mentor was right. A promoter who cancels a show at the last minute and doesn't have the courtesy to inform people who are driving hundreds of miles isn't really someone you want to be associated with, at least not on a regular basis. Plus, while I appreciated all the ring time I had gotten and the chance to work and improve in front of crowds, I never forgot that conversation I overheard during my first show.

I didn't really hold it against him. I know that many men have a body type they prefer with women. Some like muscular chicks, some like big boobs, some like waifs, and so on. When men grow up, some move on and value women for their looks, their personality, their brains, their abilities, and so on. In other words, the complete person. The ones who don't grow up continue to look at women through the eyes of adolescence. Unfortunately I was learning that wrestling was populated by a lot of promoters who were 14-year-olds inhabiting 40-year-old bodies, and in my opinion Mr. St. Jean was no exception. So, I dried my tears, put my chin up, and went back on the road. That championship belt was going to have to wait a few months before it would decorate the waist of Amanda Storm.

CHAPTER SEVENTEEN

MY SIX WEEKS AS A "WRESTLING SUPERSTAR"

STORMDATE: September to October, 1999.

In the summer of '99, I exchanged a few nice e-mails with a gal who put together and maintained a Web site for a bunch of Canadian wrestlers who all dressed like demons and vampires. The ring leader of this infernal stable of evil wrestlers worked for the Calgary-based CanAm Wrestling, a company that drove all over Canada putting on shows in bars, on Indian reservations, and other small venues. They apparently needed some wrestlers for a tour they were planning, so CanAm brought me on board for my first tour. Six weeks driving all over western Canada and wrestling just about every night. The pay wasn't going to be all that amazing, but it was a great opportunity and I seized it eagerly.

I counted down the weeks and with each passing day, the next seemed exponentially longer. It got so bad that a week before I was supposed to leave for Canada I thought and talked about little else. When the big day came I made the seven-hour drive to Montreal and caught a flight out of the Dorval airport to Calgary. From there I spent a weekend in the lovely Pointe Inn on the outskirts of Calgary.

I hung out at the bar a grand total of once the whole time I was there, and that was on the second day, when I got to meet the midgets. I didn't know that there were midgets on the tour at the time, but what were the chances of seeing not one but two midgets in the Pointe Inn and it not be related to wrestling? I am a huge fan of midgets as wrestlers and never get tired of watching their antics. It is my dream some-day to wrestle a highly skilled heel midget in a singles match.

I hate to keep calling them "the midgets" but I must con-fess that I have forgotten both of their names. Their faces are crystal clear in my mind though. One of them had short, dark hair and a very cute way of smiling that made him look very masculine and virile, and the other had long, fine blonde hair and reminded me a bit of the main character in *Raising Arizona*. He also consumed more marijuana than anyone I had ever seen — man, woman, or midget — in my life. Nice guys, and when we were on the road the blonde one taught me how to play the computer games that came with my cell phone. Before that I wasn't even aware that my cell phone had games. The things you learn on tour.

Monday came and with it so did the rest of the group. CanAm was run mainly by two gentlemen named Steve, and another guy named Otto who was basically the sergeant. I recognized the pattern immediately from my days in the military. The two Steves were the officers in charge who made the day-to-day decisions. Otto was the man who relayed the decisions to "the boys" and acted the part of good cop. He was someone the wrestlers could complain to and commiserate with in perfect safety, and for the most part Otto would sound sympathetic and let the workers vent. In doing this he was also able to gauge the morale of the troops. I could of course be reading too much into what I saw and I'm not saying that this was a deliberate arrangement, but it certainly was effective.

I piled into a big maroon van with the other wrestlers and began the long drive to our first show, which was held in an ice rink on an Indian reservation. We drove about 10 hours that day, about half of it on dirt roads that hardly could be called trails. There were deep ditches cut into either side of the road that scared us all. I thought to myself as I looked out the window, through the rain that plagued us for much of the tour, that if we slid off the road into one of these ditches, they would need a crane to pull us out.

Meanwhile to my left sat the blonde midget, oblivious to our danger, smoking a joint. His fingers flew across the keys of his cell phone as he tried to break his high score at "Snake." To my right sat a blonde babyface wrestler by the name of Gemini, who tended to rip off lines from *Austin Powers* and made a lot of the types of jokes that I won't repeat here because they are easy to take the wrong way if you hear them out of context. Gemini had a lot of natural charisma and I

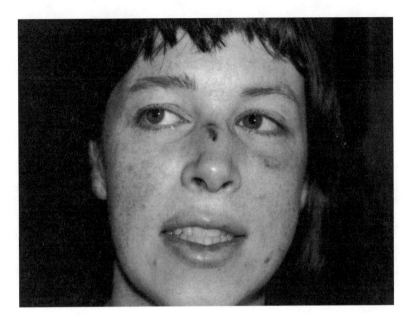

I've definitely had better days . . .
D.J. VON WYC

found it hard not to laugh at his admittedly insipid lines. He kind of reminded me of a babyface cross between David Lee Roth and Shawn Michaels.

I had my first match for CanAm, but I must confess that I don't remember most of it; my opponent and I smashed heads in the middle of the match. I don't remember how it happened or who hit whom — only that it happened. From there I went on autopilot and completed the rest of the match. I even remembered the ending where the babyface had a big comeback, climbed the top rope, and caught me with a high crossbody, only to have me roll through and reverse the pin.

Naturally I grabbed a big handful of her tights on my way to victory. At least that was what I was supposed to do.

I got my hand raised to the boo's of the crowd, and wandered off looking for the locker room. I didn't know it yet but I had a bump on my forehead the size of a small hen's egg. I was left with a big ambulance bill and a knot on my forehead that took almost six months before it entirely went away. Plus I had lost my goggles, without which I was practically blind. I wandered aimlessly and a little forlornly around the edge of the rink in my addled state, looking for a way back to the dressing room. Otto finally took me in tow and led me to the door and I descended the steps and found our room. And what did I find but my opponent laying passed out on the floor in a fetal ball. The tour had most definitely started on a rather stunning note.

The paramedics arrived and carried my opponent out on a stretcher. I was a little surprised that they insisted on doing the same with me. In retrospect I really wish I had told them to go away, because I've since gotten bills from the hospital and ambulance service that really took a bite out of what CanAm paid me for the whole tour. Such is the life of an independent wrestler.

The next day we drove another 10 hours or so to Edmonton for the next show. I broke down and found an optometrist and got some contacts on rush order. Apparently the doctor was a wrestling fan and sympathetic so he helped me out on the spot. I had avoided getting contact lenses for years because I couldn't bend my mind around the idea of sticking something in my eye. God, I was such a sissy when we did the fitting. The way I was twisting around in my chair and whining, you would have thought it was a leech on the tip of my finger instead of a contact lens. In about two hours I was scheduled to be that big, rough, badass heel wrestler, Amanda Storm, but now I was the biggest crybaby in Edmonton, Alberta, trying to avert blindness.

The grind for the next six weeks was one where we would all pile into a van and drive six to 10 hours a day to get to the next show, which would usually be in a bar or other small venue, and occasionally on a reservation. The van was pretty cramped and the spaces near the window were at a premium. Usually I ended up sitting in the back seat with a wrestler to either side of me, and surrounding myself with pillows in an effort to stay comfortable. None of the guys had really traveled with women under these circumstances before but we all quickly learned to make the best of things. It was close quarters but we all learned to worry more about being comfortable, even if it meant getting a little close at times. I spent more than a few hours kicking back with my head in Gemini's lap and vice versa but it was all totally platonic. But, hey, if you are going to share a van with a bunch of guys, it doesn't hurt if they are cute.

We'd usually arrive at our destination a few hours before the show, which would give us time to check into the hotel and drop off our things before we had to find our way to the event. From there we would catch anywhere between three and seven hours of sleep before we'd be on the road again to the next town. Occasionally we'd have a day or two off, which I took advantage of by catching up on my sleep and doing some reading. I managed to read the unabridged edition of *Don Quixote*, a couple of novels by Roger Zelazny, the Bible (twice), some of Plato's lesser known works, and various pulp fiction novels that I would find abandoned in bathrooms all across western Canada.

I had a great time overall, despite the loneliness and isolation of being on tour. This was the first time I got a taste of what life on the road must be like as a wrestling "superstar." People look at wrestlers, when they blow into town, as exciting and exotic. We are something different, a break from the monotony of everyday life. Our jobs take us all over the planet (or at least Canada) and we get to meet all sorts of different people. Unfortunately the truth of life on the road is that our relationships are superficial. We meet a lot of people but make few real friends. It is a different hotel room every night and a different town, but the same sort of drunks yelling the same tired insults. After a few weeks it becomes hard to make believe it is all fresh and new. But it is the road I chose for myself and I would definitely do it again if offered the chance.

Over the weeks I did get to see a lot of western Canada and I met some wonderful people as well as a lot of drunk ones. I worked with a number of different women and men on the tour. I thought my performances varied from somewhat unremarkable to very good at times. I was learning a lot about wrestling every night and getting good advice and feedback from veteran wrestlers like the Cuban Assassin and his son, the Cuban Assassin II. When I came back from Canada, my husband and several other people told me that I had improved a "thousand percent" as a wrestler. I don't know if this is true, but as important as wrestling school is, I think that working regularly on live shows is a very important part of a wrestler's schooling.

I also learned in a hurry that wrestling every night is different than the usual independent scene, which is a show once a month or so. You have to pace yourself when you are on tour because if Amanda Storm gets hurt, she still has to go out and perform the next three nights. Sure, if one of the guys gets hurt then he can referee or something, but CanAm had advertised a "Girl's Match" or a "Girl's Main Event" in bars all over Canada, which meant that Amanda Storm had to get in that ring *every* night, and she could do it healthy or she could do it all beat up. Either way she had to do it. So with a lot of help from the more experienced guys, I learned a lot about how to generate crowd interest and heat by using psychology and pacing instead of just throwing my body around like a crazy woman. Even so, by the end of the tour I was sore as hell and happy to be going home. Lord knows I missed my husband and was tired of reading books.

I don't want to sound like I'm bragging, but I think that I am pretty good at putting together and leading matches these days, and I think that my time at CanAm had a lot to do with this. What is more, other New England promoters were finally starting to notice me.

CHAPTER EIGHTEEN

"GET OUT THERE!"

STORMDATE: October, 1999.

I didn't have much going on after I got back from the Canada tour but I did have a couple of isolated shows with two different promoters based in Massachusetts. In one show I was standing near the curtain after heeling in what turned out to be a very good women's match. The guys were all standing around talking about what they were going to do in the upcoming battle royale. I stood staring off into space with my arms folded, wishing that I could be a part of it, and musing to myself that I was bigger than a lot of the guys who were going to be in this "slobberknocker." (Then again I wasn't exactly surrounded by wrestling mastodons either, though a couple of them were pretty impressive specimens.)

The promoter was yelling for the wrestlers to "get out there now" when a light bulb apparently went off in his head.

He looked at little Amanda standing near that curtain in her dancer leotard with the black widow she had embroidered on it a month ago in Calgary.

"Get out there," he said, smiling a little. He didn't have to tell me twice. The babyfaces were already in the ring and the heels were in the middle of charging out as a group. So I fell into the back of the pack and marched out there with the rest of them. I jumped into the ring and immediately several of the guys avoided me. Being fan favorites they didn't want to hit a woman. So I attacked one of them from behind and he turned around and just froze when he saw it was Little Amanda. I just laughed and punched him a couple of times. He staggered back and grabbed onto the ropes.

"Hit me back," I said.

"OK." He then proceeded to lay in the most tentative, weak-looking punch I had seen in my life. I shook it off, laughed and raked his eyes.

"Give me something I can sell. Forget I'm a chick." My opponent then took a swing that I knew would be stiff as hell if it connected. He certainly wasn't trying to injure me or be mean but I had gotten his dander up a little. I blocked it in the interests of self-preservation.

"Jesus. Just work with me, don't take my head off, OK?" I said, dropping down and giving him a shot between the legs.

Right about then a monstrously-huge blonde guy wearing electric blue spandex spun me around, grabbed me by the throat, and threw me into the corner. He gave me a couple of kicks and I crumpled like he had just destroyed me because

*God, how I
love a good
battle royale*
MIKE HOLMES

he was so large. I slumped in the corner for a short time and
then I rolled out of the ring to recover. Another guy was
standing near the ropes looking kind of lost.

"Baseball slide me," I said.

"What?" I couldn't say it too loud because some kids
were standing fairly close, leaning against the crowd control
barrier.

"Baseball slide me." He did and I launched myself into the
barrier. I staggered back to my feet, stunned for a moment.

222

"Again, but you'll miss."

So he did it again and I stepped to the side, grabbed his leg and half pulled him out of the ring. I proceeded to slam his leg on the apron, then grab his leg and bite him. He sat there and screamed for awhile. The kids who were standing nearby screamed obscenities at me and exhorted him to "kick my ass." Excellent. Just the reaction I had hoped for. Instead he rolled back into the ring and staggered to his feet.

I could see that the heels were getting thrown out of the ring, so I didn't go back in. Instead I grabbed a chair that one of the fans had slid toward the ring. I had a dual purpose. My main reason was to get a potentially dangerous piece of debris out of the way so none of the wrestlers stumbled over it and got hurt. Plus I thought it might look good to stalk around with a chair and look mean. I paused to rip the athletic tape from around my wrist. It had come undone and the loose end was flopping around when I waved my arm. I promptly threw it in the face of a young man who was screaming that I was a bitch. I asked him if the even younger man standing next to him was his girlfriend.

One of the security guys was trying to get the heels into the back so the babyfaces could leave the ring and the show could move on to the main event. He was having some problems getting them to cooperate without being obvious to the fans. So I stalked back through the curtain very happy with the small role I had played in my first battle royale.

The most important thing from this show was I got a chance to meet one Steve Ricard, who was the booker for

South Coast Championship Wrestling, a small federation that runs shows mainly in southeastern Massachusetts. Steve is the first person who gave me a chance to work every week as a wrestler, often two and three shows in a weekend. What is more, Ricard started having me work mixed matches against a wide variety of opponents. The most fun I've had so far as a wrestler without a doubt has been working for this promotion.

I started out with Steve as a heel, and I don't think there are too many women in wrestling who are able to work effectively as a heel in a back-and-forth match with a man who outweighs her by about a hundred pounds, comes to the ring wearing a black trenchcoat and a mask, and does a Satanic gimmick. But I had such a match with a guy named Matt Storm for South Coast not too long ago.

Mostly I wrestle guys who are about my size or perhaps a little smaller. Over the months something happened that I never would have expected. Amanda Storm became a Babyface Blakwidow. We were wrestling in the same bars and legion halls week after week, and I made it a point to work on as many of these shows as possible. I think that the fans found my heel antics funny and when we gave them an excuse to start cheering me instead of booing, the people were ready. So it was a whole new way of thinking about a wrestling match for me, because I was handing out candy to the people instead of trying to steal it.

I feel like I took two steps backwards as a wrestler in terms of skill when I switched to wrestling as a fan favorite. Almost all of my training, my move set, and my experience was geared towards being a villain. But Steve was patient with me and I have slowly improved in my new role.

I teamed up with Don Juan DeSanto early on to feud with Chris Blackheart and "Gorgeous" Gino Giovanni, who is one of the best-groomed straight men I know. I have had four very punishing matches with one Edward G. Xstacy, who is a 250-pound powerlifter and in the ring is an invertebrate misogynist. Then there is the 270-pound, leather-clad Trent MacNeely, who wouldn't look out of place as one of the Village People. He has the annoying habit of putting me in a full nelson and swinging me around and around, finally throwing me half away across the ring before pinning my poor carcass.

Lately I've battled Vertebreaker, who rather reminds me of a good-natured but evil face-painted troll who slaps on 20 pounds of duct tape every match to brace his injuries. Then there is little Mike Paiva, who has the distinction of being the only wrestler Amanda Storm has ever pressed over her head in a live match.

These are just a few of the wrestlers I've worked with and I wish I could mention them all. In any case, I am very lucky to have stumbled upon a promotion where I have found a wrestling home almost every weekend. And what is more I am starting to make appearances wrestling men in other New England federations, mainly because some of the wrestlers I work with are saying nice things about me to the bookers in other places they work. And for that I am most grateful and heartened that I apparently am earning the respect of my peers.

CHAPTER NINETEEN

BUT DON'T TAKE MY WORD FOR IT

While I was working on this book I had a chance to speak with other wrestlers about their experiences. Chris Bundy and Rick Martel were kind enough to share their views about the life, and I thought their inclusion here might offer a different perspective on what I've been writing about for the last 220 pages.

RICK MARTEL

Rick Martel put in an appearance at Killer Kowalski's one fine summer evening in 1999 talking to the students and answering our questions. He was kind enough to give me permission to repeat some of what he said here in my book. He told me to "use my discretion" and that he "trusted me" when I made the decision what to write and what to keep quiet. I can only say that I did my best and I hope, Mr. Martel, if you read this, that you are pleased or at least not appalled. I must say that in meeting him, I found Rick to be fun, soft-spoken, full of wonderful advice, and quite a gentleman.

When he visited, Rick was cutting back on wrestling but was doing French commentary for WCW.

QUESTION: How do you get up for a performance where there are only 25 fans?

RICK: I worked in front of small crowds early in my career and I always tried to give my best each and every time. You never know who is watching a show, no matter how small the audience or how isolated the venue. You never know who people talk to either. You could wrestle in front of 25 people but one of those people could know someone in the WWF, talk to them, and before you know it you're getting a phone call.

QUESTION: What if a promoter asks you to come across to the fans in a way you don't like or gives you a role you don't enjoy?

RICK: It is important to be flexible and there is often a silver lining in what seem like bad situations. I have been in situations in my career that didn't seem very good at first, but I gave it a try and good things happened. Try to find the positive and be open to new ideas and giving them a go. You might be pleasantly surprised by the results.

QUESTION: What if you don't like how the promoter uses you in the shows?

RICK: Your attitude and reputation are extremely important aspects of whether or not you will be successful in the long-term as a wrestler. Promoters will often test you by asking you to do things that aren't necessarily glamorous to see how you react. And bookers talk to each other about wrestlers' attitudes, just as wrestlers will talk to other wrestlers about promoters. Nothing will kill you faster in this business than having a poor attitude or a big ego.

QUESTION: What are some of the most important aspects for making it as a wrestler?

RICK: Go to the gym. How you look is very important. You don't necessarily have to be a muscle man or woman, but you should try to look athletic and if possible larger than life. People are paying to see someone who is out of the ordinary, not someone who looks like they could have just walked off the street and jumped into the ring. Obviously wrestling ability is important. Take the time to train at a good wrestling school and learn the basics. Don't just concentrate on the big moves that impress the fans. Take the time to become a complete wrestler. Third, and especially these days, it is important to be at home in front of the camera and with a microphone. Practice your interview skills as diligently as you go to the gym and train in the ring. All three are important to your success.

QUESTION: How hard is being a full-time wrestler in a federation like WCW on one's family life?

RICK: The time on the road associated with working full-time can take a tremendous toll on your family. Although we are all professional wrestlers, it is important to remember that family is more important. A lot of wrestlers make the mistake of not leaving wrestling when they are at home. They love the sport and live it 24/7. Unfortunately this may not be the case for your wife, girlfriend, or boyfriend. Try to live a balanced life of which wrestling is only one and certainly not the most important aspect.

KING KONG BUNDY

If you've gotten this far, you know that I think King Kong "Call Me Chris" Bundy is the stone groove. I had the opportunity not too long ago to speak with him on the phone.

AMANDA: Are you married?

CHRIS: Yes, but you already know that.

AMANDA: What was your greatest moment in wrestling?

CHRIS: That's hard to say, there have been so many. I'd have to say wrestling Hulk Hogan in Wrestlemania II for the WWF title in 1986.

AMANDA: How did you happen to get into pro wrestling?

CHRIS: It was 1981 and I was broke. I was going to buy a Mexican restaurant and the deal fell through. I was drifting around tending bar at the time. My brother was teaching elementary PE and the father of one of his student's dads was a referee for the WWF. I asked my brother about getting some tickets to the WWF show, which was coming to town. Somehow the message got mixed up and the dad was told I wanted to be a wrestler.

AMANDA: Who trained you?

CHRIS: I was trained by Larry Sharpe at the Monster Factory.

AMANDA: How did you come up with the name "King Kong Bundy"? Is that your real name?

CHRIS: Oh, Amanda, call me Chris. I was working down in Knoxsville, Tennessee, as Big Daddy Bundy and they billed me as a babyface from the Texas oil fields. There were 27 Von Erichs down there, so I switched to a heel because I had no future as a face. Fritz Von Erich didn't think that "Big Daddy" sounded good for a heel, so I became King Kong Bundy.

AMANDA: Who have been some of your influences in wrestling?

CHRIS: I talked to a lot of guys in the WWF. Hulk Hogan, the Magnificent Muraco, and Rick Martel all come to mind.

AMANDA: Rick is a super nice guy.

CHRIS: Yes, he is. A super talent as a face or heel, he had the look, the fire, and could do it all.

AMANDA: What do you like most about wrestling?

CHRIS: Well, it is a job but I meet a lot of nice people in my travels, which I have to say is the best thing about wrestling.

AMANDA: What are some of the things you dislike about wrestling?

CHRIS: The travel can be tough, but as much as I bitch about it I can't think of anything else I'd rather do. I've done a lot of crazy things, but like Hillybilly Jim said, "Hey, you can send me out there in a greenbean suit. I threw out my pride in wrestling a long time ago." Like everyone though, I dislike the politics and the kindergarten bullshit and egos about something that is supposed to be a work. There are a lot of nice people in wrestling but for every nice person there are 836 boneheads. You can't swing a dead cat in wrestling without hitting a bonehead.

AMANDA: I know what you mean.

CHRIS: One time we were wrestling the Killer Bees, Jim Brunzell and B. Brian Blair. We were coming back in another show against Andre the Giant and Black Jack Mulligan, who was 6′ 9″ and 310 pounds. But Brunzell and Blair wouldn't job, even though it would have made sense to build us up for the match down the road against a couple of monsters. It would have just made good business sense.

AMANDA: Sounds like it would have indeed. Speaking of large, powerful people, what are your stats, Chris?

CHRIS: I'm 6′ 4″ and 425 pounds. I was about 445 pounds when I was in the WWF.

AMANDA: Nice. What is your favorite move?

CHRIS: I'd have to say my finisher, the Avalanche, where I'd squash guys in the corner. It was certified and tested in a lab as exerting 83,791 pounds per square inch.

AMANDA: That's a lot of pounds. Certified and everything, wow. Does wrestling take a toll on your personal life?

CHRIS: No, I don't really think so. It was tough on my first marriage but that would have ended anyway. As for now, I'm gone a lot but as they say, "Absence makes the heart grow fonder."

AMANDA: What are you doing in wrestling now?

CHRIS: I'm working in a lot of the indie feds and doing personal appearances. If there is a payday, I'm there.

AMANDA: How about outside of wrestling?

CHRIS: Nothing. Wrestling is my life right now.

AMANDA: What are your plans for the future? How much longer do you see yourself in wrestling?

CHRIS: Maybe opening a wrestling school. I see the really old guys working and think, "What the hell is he doing?" but at the same time I understand that people have to make a living. A couple of years maybe, but probably as long as I can. Fifty maybe. Whatever I can do to make the most money. If I can make more as a security guard at Sears then I'll do that. I like wrestling, but if you *have* to be someplace then it's work.

AMANDA: Where can people go to check out your Web site?

CHRIS: It is www.kingkongbundy.com.

AMANDA: Thank you so much, Chris, it was really nice talking with you.

CHRIS: The pleasure was all mine.

EPILOGUE

SUBLIMINAL MESSAGE #13:
HIRE ME VINCE!

STORMDATE: August, 2000.

How do you end a story that is in fact (hopefully) just beginning? This is a hard book to end because every weekend is a new adventure and potentially a new chapter. Just this last weekend I was the flag-waving, glasses-wearing Amanda "Miss USA" Storm from Union City, New Jersey, wrestling the evil British girl, Felicity, at a car dealership in my "hometown" for Bob Fury's promotion. Bob told me that the show was a great success and they sold six cars because of the wrestlers.

A couple of days later I was fighting Felicity again, but this time she was the good girl Canadian heroine and we were in Montreal. I was still Miss USA, but I was the all-American girl with a bad attitude yet again for Jacques Rougeau's Lutte Internationale 2000. I rode a $40,000 customized Harley out to the ring with 3,500 fans screaming at me in French as I grabbed the mike and cut another one of my "Canada Sucks" promos. Plus Mr. Rougeau had taken time before the match, as he always has in the past, to help make Amanda a better wrestler. This time he invited me to come up a few days early to his wrestling school for his December 2000 extravaganza. I see this as an honor and in my opinion Jacques is an incredible teacher and a wrestling genius. Plus the mark in me just loves taking bumps and learning moves and psychology from "The Mountie." It all makes me glad that I'm Amanda Storm.

Plus I have gone from wrestling once every couple of months for a promoter who was disappointed that my tits were too small to wrestling two or even three times a weekend. Steve Ricard of South Coast Championship Wrestling has been providing me with ring time wrestling a variety of male opponents literally every week for months now. And wrestling men in good, credible-looking matches has gotten me a lot of publicity, too. Just last weekend, when I was in New Jersey, I was interviewed about wrestling men by the New York correspondent for O Globo, which is a Brazilian newspaper.

The thing that makes me happiest about the mixed matches is that the guys are actually asking to wrestle me now. When I first started doing them it was always, "I have to wrestle a woman?" But in taking the same bumps, doing jobs for the guys, and showing up to all of the small shows, I think that I have earned their respect as someone who wants the same thing they do, which is a chance to perform in front of the fans and earn the title of being a "worker" from my peers.

Amanda hangs out with the women's champ
D.J. VON WYC

Plus I get plenty of matches now against a variety of female opponents, and am doing my best to build a good reputation with the other gals.

I think the strangest and most unexpected thing to come my way in wrestling lately is that I am actually getting more wrestling time now as a babyface. I know that prancing around like a sycophantic good girl with a stupid smile on her face isn't exactly good for the "Blakwidow" image I have tried so hard to build, but a girl has to do what a girl has to do. I enjoy the challenge of being the gal who hands out the wrestling candy instead of stealing it, and as the fans come to recognize me and as I practice this role more and more, it becomes easier with each performance.

SUBLIMINAL MESSAGE #13: HIRE ME VINCE!

I have also done color commentary for Ultimate Professional Wrestling's television show, which I am told is shown over much of the country. I have been asked for my ideas about angles and finishes at wrestling events and little Amanda has even been the booker for one fed. Within the next year I will probably be teaming up with some people to help promote my own shows in New England. All in all much has happened to me in my second year that I wasn't able to write about here since this book is mainly about my first year as a pro wrestler. If my little effort is as successful as I hope (buy my book please!) then perhaps I will be lucky enough to start work on the sequel. Perhaps the title will be: *Amanda Storm — My Life as an All-American Stereotype*.

Speaking of publicity, the Jim Gerard article finally came out in the September 2000 anniversary edition of *Penthouse* magazine. It brought back a lot of memories of my earliest struggles to break into wrestling and the crazy lengths I was willing to go to in order to be a part of wrestling shows. Yes, back then I was willing to drive 10 hours for $25. It all seems so long ago now . . .

I was very excited about the article and to date this is the biggest piece of publicity (besides this book of course) to come my way. I was a bit surprised that they mentioned I was bisexual and I have gotten a ton of e-mail about this. Much of it consists of pictures of cute young women who seem to be looking at me as some sort of role model, which comes as a complete surprise. But mainly people want to know if this little tidbit about my sexual orientation is true. All I will say

The belt right where it belongs. Looks good, don't you think?
D.J. VON WYC

here is that I am not going to say. In a sport where the endings are pre-determined, I would prefer to retain this small element of mystery.

In a sense seeing the article in print and completing this book gives me a warm feeling of closure. I have put the struggles of my first year behind me: My battles outside the ring and disagreements with a couple of wrestlers, unscrupulous and adolescent promoters, the difficulty in getting wrestling training and uprooting our lives, and not least the bruises, injuries, and pain that is a constant reality for every professional wrestler who is worth his or her salt. A lot of wonderful things have happened to me and I look forward to the next year with hope. I was told that some scouts for a major federation came to a show I was on recently and liked what they saw. And I plan on asking Mr. Kowalski to take me with him backstage when Vince puts in his next appearance at the Fleet Center in Boston. Maybe he'll like me and maybe I'll get to finally meet HHH. (I'll have to remember to stay cool and not act too much like the mark that throbs inside the heart of every active wrestler.)

For what it is worth, I never did win that women's title from Violet, because we both stopped working for the promotion the show before I was slated to win the thing. She has since moved with her husband out to Arizona, which put a bit of a damper on our bouts. But in the past few months I've more than made up for this travesty of wrestling justice and definitely won my share of New England gold. The following championships have come my way in the past few months: Ultimate Professional Wrestling Women's Title (Maine); South Coast Championship Wrestling Women's Title (New England); SCCW Interstate Title (New England); National Wrestling Alliance of New England Women's Title (three times); Main Event Wrestling Cruiserweight Title (Vermont); Dragon Crown Wrestling Women's Title (New England); South Coast Championship Wrestling Universal Champion; and Yankee Pro Wrestling Women's Title (New England).

Until that second book comes out, if you want to continue following the trials and tribulations, the travails and triumphs of Amanda Storm, then you can always visit my Web site at www.blakwidow.com and join my free Internet e-mail list by dropping me a line at storm@blakwidow.com. Now that you have read my book, look at this last page not as the ending but as the beginning, an introduction if you will. If luck goes my way then perhaps in the very near future you will be seeing a lot more of Amanda Storm on your television set or at a show in a city, town, bar, auditorium, fair, or car dealership near you.

Blessed Be,

"The Blakwidow"